CHARACTERS

(in order of their appearance)

Mrs Tadwich
Simon Sparrow
Wildewinde
Sir Lancelot Spratt, F.R.C.S.
Grimsdyke
Delivery Man
Mr Claribold
Kitten
Nikki
Florence Nightingale

SYNOPSIS OF SCENES

The action of the play passes in the consulting room of Dr Sparrow's practice at Hampden Cross, a market town in Hampshire

ACT I

A summer morning

ACT II

One o'clock in the morning, a fortnight later

Time—the present

ACT I

SCENE—*Dr Sparrow's consulting room. A morning in summer.*

This is a converted downstairs room in a pleasant old house, giving the impression of modern medicine practised efficiently in agreeable though somewhat museum-like surroundings. The main door, leading to the hall, is up L. *A long bow window up* C, *with net curtains, looks out on to the garden, to the left of which the exterior wall of the house, containing the front door, runs off at a right-angle. A smaller door up* R *leads to a narrow staircase twisting its way upstairs. Below this door is a glass and metal surgery cupboard containing a jumble of books, dressings and instruments, then a rather elegant wash-basin with a surgical tap, operated by the elbow, and finally an electric sterilizer on a shelf, which also contains enamel dishes and instruments. Underneath are the doctor's bag and a pedal-operated dressing-bin. An examination couch, shielded by a curtain on runners, stands* L *with a radiant heat lamp below it. The doctor's desk is* R, *with his chair behind it. A chair for patients is* L *of the desk. A half-folded Chinese screen stands up* R. *Other clinical apparatus, such as a weighing-machine and a height-measure, may be added if wished. Before the* CURTAIN *rises, a telephone is heard ringing, joined after a moment by a second one. To this is added an urgent intermittent buzzing from an intercom.*

When the CURTAIN *rises,* SIMON, *stethoscope in hand, is leaping from the direction of the examination couch, which is curtained, towards the telephones and intercom on the desk. He is dressed fairly informally for a general practitioner.*

MRS TADWICH (*behind the curtain; huskily*) But, Doctor—do you want me to take everything off?

SIMON (*over his shoulder; hastily*) Yes, please. (*Very hustled, he grabs both telephones at once. He speaks into the right-hand telephone first*) Hello? Yes? This is the doctor. (*Into the left-hand telephone*) Hello? Dr Simon Sparrow speaking. . . . The *new* doctor. . . . What's that? Wait a second while I find a pencil. (*With both telephones held by his hunched-up shoulders, he struggles to take a pencil from his inside pocket and a note-pad from the desk*)

MRS TADWICH (*behind the curtain*) What, *the lot?*

SIMON (*towards the screen; briefly*) Yes, please. (*To himself*) You can keep your ear-rings on. (*Into the left-hand telephone*) Now, what's the trouble?

(*A dress is flung across the top of the curtain rail.* SIMON *struggles to write on the pad, repeating tonelessly the message as received*)

"Gran's took queer again, but this time it's different."

(*The inter-com buzzes loudly several times.* SIMON *glares at it*)

What's Gran look like? (*Into the right-hand telephone*) Yes, I *am* listening. (*Into the left-hand telephone*) Hang on. (*Into the right-hand telephone, again repeating the message tonelessly*) "The baby's eaten Mum's oral contraceptives."

(*A pair of stockings join the dress across the rail*)

Well, I shouldn't think it'll matter. Not to the baby, at any rate. (*Into the left-hand telephone*) *Where* do you say gran's locked in? You could try getting through the window, couldn't you? I *know* it's got a very small window. They always *have* a very small window.

(*A flimsy girdle joins the stockings*)

Well, call the fire brigade, or something. It's *their* job, not mine. (*He continues into the right-hand telephone*) No, no! Don't *you* call the fire brigade.

(*A brief bra joins the other clothes. The intercom gives another blast of urgent buzzes.* SIMON *speaks into both telephones at once*)

I'll come as soon as I can. (*He replaces both telephones, presses the switch of the intercom, and speaks in its direction*) Wildewinde! Come to the surgery at once. I *know* you're cooking lunch. I don't care if the soufflé *doesn't* rise. I don't care if it explodes in your face. This is an emergency. (*He makes towards the couch*)

(*A miniscule pair of black white-edged panties misses its perch on the rail and falls at his feet. He picks them up with a look of resignation*)

MRS TADWICH (*putting her head and bare shoulders through the curtain, revealing that she is an attractive, if rather weird, young lady. Her straight hair drops from her fringe perpendicularly to her shoulders, and she is made up startlingly. Her attitude is self-dramatic*) I'm ready for you to sense my vibrations, Doctor.

SIMON (*flustered*) Not—not for a minute, Mrs Tadwich.

MRS TADWICH (*surprised*) But I can't take anything *else* off.

SIMON. I've got to wait for a chaperone.

MRS TADWICH (*more surprised*) At your age?

SIMON. Perhaps you'll allow me to explain the rules of medical ethics? A doctor should *never* examine a lady patient between the clavicles and the patella—(*explaining*)—the kneecap—unless in the presence of another female.

MRS TADWICH (*looking lost*) Whatever for?

SIMON. Because—because it's the rule.

MRS TADWICH (*co-operative*) But *I* don't mind! (*Her leg appears as she is about to leave the curtain, and we see she wears an enormous gold scorpion charm round her neck*)

SIMON (*hastily motioning her back*) I—I'll see it all in a minute. (*Noticing the charm blankly*) What on earth's that lobster doing?

MRS TADWICH. I'm scorpio, Doctor. I wear it to keep *my* vibrations in tune with the universe.

Simon (*indicating inside the screen*) Just slip that gown thing round your—vibrations, please.

(Mrs Tadwich *disappears, and* Wildewinde, *a motherly little middle-aged man in a short white jacket, bustles in from the main door up* L)

Wildewinde. Here I am, Doctor! (*Rubbing his hands*) Where's the emergency?

Simon. I want you to hold the ring while I look at Mrs Tadwich.

(Wildewinde's *face falls with disappointment.* Mrs Tadwich *appears statuesquely from the curtain in a short towelling dressing-gown*)

Mrs Tadwich. I thought you said in the presence of another *female?*

Simon (*briefly*) This is the best I can do. Mr Wildewinde—with two "es"—is our long-established general factotum. Ex-ship's steward.

Wildewinde (*proudly*) In the *Queen Mary*, madam.

Simon. Now. (*He moves the chair in front of the desk to face up stage*) I want you in a good light, please.

(Mrs Tadwich *sits on the chair facing the window, while* Simon *sternly indicates* Wildewinde *to retire to the corner down* R, *then continues in a very business-like tone*)

Simon. How long have you been married?

Mrs Tadwich. There's a divorce pending. My husband's vibrations and my own *clashed.*

Simon (*slipping his stethoscope round his neck; off-handedly*) A pity.

Mrs Tadwich. You see, my vibrations are *so strong.* And his were the wobbling of a *jelly.* Do *you* consult the stars, Doctor?

Simon. I don't think that would be very popular with the medical authorities, either.

Mrs Tadwich. I never make a move without reading my horoscope. It told me today I was going to meet—(*looking at him meanfully*)—some *very* sympathetic vibrations.

Simon (*puzzled*) Mrs Tadwich, you mean you feel the actual *vibrations* in your chest?

Mrs Tadwich (*indicating the middle of her chest with a sweeping gesture*) *Here!* Like a *bird* fluttering.

Simon (*placing his hand on the afflicted area*) Ah, yes! I feel a distinct thrill.

Mrs Tadwich (*quietly gratified*) Doctor! I said you'd vibrate too.

Simon (*leaping away in horror*) Mrs Tadwich! I didn't mean *that* at all! It's just a doctor's name for a certain—quivering sensation.

Mrs Tadwich (*very huskily*) And mine.

(*A telephone rings.* Wildewinde *answers it.* Simon *ushers* Mrs Tandwich *towards the couch again. She disappears behind the curtain, which* Simon *pulls firmly across*)

WILDEWINDE (*into the telephone*) Dr Sparrow's consulting rooms . . . This is Wildewinde, your Ladyship . . . Yes, indeed. I'll tell the doctor at once. Thank you for operating the early warning system, your Ladyship. (*He replaces the telephone*)

(*The clothes are all whisked off the top of the curtain-rail*)

SIMON (*hopelessly, sinking on the window-seat*) At least nothing worse than *that* can happen to me today.

WILDEWINDE (*approaching*) I'm afraid it can, Doctor. Lady Spratt was on the telephone. Sir Lancelot is paying you a call, and will be here at any moment.

SIMON (*leaping up again*) Oh, no! (*Starts pacing the room in agitation*) Why—why!—with the whole world open to him from Alaska to Australia must the old dragon retire in this particular town?

WILDEWINDE. I fancy he finds the local angling a great attraction, Doctor.

SIMON (*moving up and down* C) I wouldn't mind if he confined himself to pestering the fish. Just as I was congratulating myself on qualifying, and escaping from our *venerated* senior surgeon at St Swithin's for good and all, I find I'm sharing the same telephone directory with him. (*Very determinedly*) I'm not going to see him! It's only a social call. I shall be "not at home". Wildewinde, you will answer the door and say that Dr Sparrow is definitely not—at—home. . . .

(SIMON *trails off as he notices* SIR LANCELOT's *face glaring through the window*)

SIR LANCELOT. Don't stand there looking as useless as an udder on a bull! Open up! (*He disappears towards the front door*)

SIMON (*with a hopeless motion*) You'd better let him in.

WILDEWINDE (*making for the door*) Oh, dear! The soufflé!

(SIMON *stands at the chair behind the desk. As* WILDEWINDE *opens the door,* SIR LANCELOT *enters* L. *He is a fierce, burly, bearded figure in tweeds and a hat decorated with fishing flies. He holds a buff card and is in a bad temper.*

WILDEWINDE, *with an apprehensive look, slips from the room behind his back, closing the door*)

SIR LANCELOT. 'Morning, Sparrow. Finished your day's work, I see.

SIMON (*respectful, in spite of himself*) It's almost my lunch hour, Sir Lancelot. Or my lunch half-hour, rather. So if you could make your —(*with a weak smile*)—friendly visit fairly brief . . .

SIR LANCELOT (*sitting sideways on the chair* L *of the desk*) It isn't a friendly visit. It's a professional one.

SIMON (*sitting above the desk; puzzled*) But I didn't want your opinion on anything?

SIR LANCELOT. No, but I want yours. I'm coming on your list as a patient. National Health Service, of course. None of these damn private fees for me. There's my card. (*He tosses a Health Card on the desk*)

SIMON. But what about your own doctor?

SIR LANCELOT. That man isn't fit to doctor a tom-cat. Can't diagnose a simple case of lumbago. Besides you're more convenient for the river.

SIMON (*another weak smile expressing his inadequacy*) But I can't take clinical responsibility for *you*, Sir Lancelot.

SIR LANCELOT. I don't want you to take responsibility for anything. I've got a ghastly attack of lumbago. Came on after breakfast, when I was having a bit of a tiff with the missus. I want a prescription. Two prescriptions. One for embrocation, one for some codeine.

SIMON. I see. (*After a pause*) But I shall have to examine you first.

SIR LANCELOT (*outraged*) Examine me? What are you trying to say, boy? That I don't recognize my own lumbago when I feel it?

SIMON (*determinedly and calmly as possible*) The decision to prescribe drugs should be entirely your doctor's responsibility, arrived at after careful examination . . .

SIR LANCELOT. Who put ideas like that in your head?

SIMON. You did. For years you drummed into us at St Swithin's that every patient must be *properly examined*. Even if it meant stripping a duchess to the buff in a horse-box.

SIR LANCELOT (*his tone turning to quiet menace as he half-slips off his jacket and makes for the curtain*) Very well! Examine me you shall. And you had better be good!

(SIR LANCELOT *sweeps back the curtain revealing* MRS TADWICH, *fully if weirdly dressed, but doing up her suspender. She screams.* SIMON *who had totally forgotten her, rushes round the desk with a look of horror*)

SIR LANCELOT (*fiercely*) Really, Sparrow! Your practice may be busy, but it's no excuse for keeping your patients double-parked.

SIMON (*hastening Mrs Tadwich out*) One of my heart cases.

SIR LANCELOT. I have no doubt.

SIMON (*to Mrs Tadwich*) If you kindly wait outside I'll see you when I've dealt with this patient.

MRS TADWICH (*huskily*) I'm vibrating *all over*, Doctor . . .

(SIMON *shows* MRS TADWICH *out.* SIR LANCELOT *has been taking all this in silently, still with his jacket half off*)

SIR LANCELOT. What exactly is your relationship with that over-perfumed witch?

SIMON. The—er, usual doctor-patient relationship.

(SIR LANCELOT *takes off his jacket and pulls up his back shirt-tail, leaning on the couch as* SIMON *starts examining his lumbar region*)

SIR LANCELOT. Hm. I suppose you know your medical ethics in a nutshell, don't you? It's perfectly all right to make your mistress one of your patients. But it certainly *isn't* all right to make your patients mistresses.

SIMON (*shocked*) There's nothing in the slightest like that! (*Poking him*) Does that hurt?

SIR LANCELOT (*giving a loud yell*) Yes! Look here, my boy—how much do you know about women?

SIMON. Well—I dissected one once.

SIR LANCELOT. I suppose you're aware the local G.P. is a sitting target for every frustrated housewife in the practice? And about half the unfrustrated ones, too, in my calculation.

SIMON (*primly*) I think I am quite able to look after myself, thank you, Sir Lancelot. (*Prodding*) How about that?

SIR LANCELOT (*giving a louder yell*) I doubt it very much. You must get a wife. (*The examination over, he starts dressing*) Besides, the men patients expect it. They don't like the doctor messing about with their wives unless they know he's got one of his own at home.

SIMON. The operation might be rather difficult. I don't seem to know any girls.

SIR LANCELOT (*impatiently*) Oh, come, boy! A lot of young women would break a leg to marry the local doctor. (*Reflecting*) Quite a number of them do.

(*A telephone rings*)

SIMON (*moving behind the desk*) Excuse me. (*Into the telephone*) Dr Sparrow here. . . . Your husband's got it stuck *where?* . . . I shouldn't think he *could* get it out. That's what vacuum cleaners are for. Have you tried switching off the current? . . . Well, I should. (*Replacing the telephone; to Sir Lancelot*) The places people *will* put their fingers.

SIR LANCELOT (*sitting in the patient's chair*) You would seem to be somewhat under-staffed.

SIMON (*sitting behind the desk; resignedly*) *Am* I! This is really a three-doctor practice, what with the other surgery across the town and all our clinic work. But you know what happened—soon after I arrived a month ago, Dr Farquarson went into hospital himself, poor chap, with a duodenal. Then Dr Cooper upped sticks and emigrated to Australia. Can't say I blame him. Now they've abolished the prescription charges, being a doctor in the National Health Service is like running a supermarket without a cash desk.

SIR LANCELOT. Haven't you discovered yet, young man, the British public never feel healthy unless it's taking loads of medicine?

SIMON. Then Miss Frisby, our dear old receptionist—a State-registered nurse—inherited a small fortune from her brother and took herself off to Bournemouth.

(*The other telephone rings*)

(*Curtly, into it*) Who is it? . . . Oh! Yes, of course. (*His manner becomes very respectful. He covers the mouthpiece. To Sir Lancelot*) One of our few private patients. (*Into the telephone*) Hello, Lady Forcebrace. And how are *you* this morning? . . . I'm *so* glad it's better. And the Field-Marshal—how is his gout? . . . He's *what?* Been run over by his own lawn-mower? That's a bit off for a master of tank tactics, isn't it? . . .

(*Alarmed*) Oh, no, Lady Forcebrace, I wasn't being funny . . . I'm sure it's very painful—particularly just there . . . I'll be over as soon as poss . . . (*He discovers the line is dead, and with a shrug puts it down*)

Sir Lancelot. But can't you find a couple of locums and a nurse?

Simon (*getting up and wandering about hopelessly*) Impossible! Absolutely impossible. At this time of the year, every doctor in the country seems to be going on holiday. They're *all* wanting locums. I've advertised in both medical journals. I've written to the medical agencies.

(*The telephone rings*)

(*Answering it*) Dr Sparrow. . . . No, madam, I do *not* write prescriptions for budgies. (*He replaces it*) I even had a notice stuck on the board at St Swithin's Hospital—at least that produced *one* chap, though very temporary.

Sir Lancelot. Then where is he?

Simon. He had to go to London yesterday to get some new instruments. (*Looking at his watch*) He ought to be back. He's supposed to be taking *this* surgery. (*Remembering*) By the way, it *is* lumbago.

Sir Lancelot. I am extremely gratified your ham-fisted examination led you to the diagnosis I already provided. (*Getting up*) Well, I can't waste all morning here. The fish'll be rising. Where's my prescriptions?

(Simon *scribbles on a pad and tears off two sheets.* Sir Lancelot *takes them*)

Sir Lancelot. I expect someone else will turn up to give you a hand. (*Kindly*) I don't want to see you tumbling base over apex into an early grave through overwork.

Simon (*touched*) It's very kind of you to think of my health, Sir Lancelot.

Sir Lancelot (*his usual self again*) It's not *your* blasted health I'm thinking of. It's mine. If there aren't any decent doctors in this town, at least I'm going to pick one I trained personally. Good morning!

(Sir Lancelot *moves to the door up* L. Wildewinde *enters with a handful of letters.* Sir Lancelot *sniffs*)

Wildewinde. My after-shave.

(Sir Lancelot *grunts and leaves.* Wildewinde *crosses to the desk*)

The second post, Doctor.

Simon (*sorting the letters eagerly*) Drug circular—circular—subscription to the cricket club—overdraft—and not a damn reply from those medical employment agencies! By the way, I've got to dash out on a case.

Wildewinde. If I may remind you, Doctor, there's still a gentleman and that peculiar lady Mrs Tadwich in the waiting-room.

Simon (*opening an envelope*) I can't help that. Our Field-Marshal has been mown down in action. (*He glances at his watch*)

Wildewinde (*tragically*) And my soufflé, Doctor!

SIMON. I'll eat it for supper. With chips. No sign of my partner yet, is there?

WILDEWINDE. I fear Dr Grimsdyke is *very* irregular in his habits . . .

SIMON. Hey! Listen to this. We've got a bite. (*Reading from a hand-written letter*) "Dear Dr Sparrow, I have just heard from a contact at St Swithin's Hospital"—that'll be my notice—"that you are looking for a locum tenens. I should be glad if you would consider me for the post, as I wish to get some experience of family doctoring before specializing . . ." (*To Wildewinde*) Specializing! He must be intelligent. (*Reading*) "I am fully qualified, aged twenty-three, unmarried, and I have a car. I would like to call on you during the morning of the fifteenth, and unless I hear to the contrary I shall assume . . ." The fifteenth! That's today. (*Peering at the letter*) It was posted a week ago! Wildewinde . . . ?

WILDEWINDE. I fear I have been getting a touch forgetful of late. We all have our little failings.

SIMON (*glaring at him, and resuming the letter*) "I hope you will find me a satisfactory and willing worker, and I assure you that I shall do my best to please." Signed—(*peering*)—"Nicholas Barrington". Well, I've never heard of the fellow, but at least he sounds clean and sober.

(*Through the door up* L *bounds* GRIMSDYKE. *He is a gay, sporty young man with an eye for girls of all ages and social or professional status. He is dressed more fashionably than Simon, and wears a ridiculously up-to-the-moment hat, which he tosses on to the window-seat. He has under his arm a flat cardboard box tied with string*)

GRIMSDYKE. 'Ullo, 'ullo, 'ullo! Sorry I'm late. Thanks, Simon, for looking after the shop.

SIMON (*interested, but also rather annoyed*) Where on earth did you get to?

GRIMSDYKE (*sitting nonchalantly in the patient's chair*) Afraid I rather overslept, old lad.

SIMON (*looking at his watch*) You certainly did! I hope she wasn't late for work, too.

GRIMSDYKE (*airily*) Come, come! Wildewinde, mix me a refreshing vodka and lime, will you? I've got a tongue like a pub doormat.

WILDEWINDE (*to himself; shocked*) Vodka! (*Moving up* L) In the surgery! Certainly not!

(WILDEWINDE *exits up* L)

SIMON. I've had one bit of good news. We're not going to be rushed off our feet any more.

GRIMSDYKE. You've found a locum?

SIMON. Yes. Young chap, unmarried, called Nicholas Barrington. Seems keen.

GRIMSDYKE. Spendid! We can sling the dirty work on him. (*Rubbing his hands*) All those night calls! All those week-ends! All the neurotics with nothing wrong with them! Oh, and the inquests!

Always give me the creeps, inquests. (*Struck by an alarming thought*)
I hope this Barrington fellow's going to be normal. Chases women,
that sort of thing?

SIMON (*inspecting the letter again*) The handwriting looks a bit
prissy.

GRIMSDYKE. We'll soon get him trained. (*Rising*) Well, Simon,
congratulate yourself—the practice is now fully and permanently up
to strength.

SIMON. But you're only helping out for a few weeks—as an old
pal. Until that millionaire's private physician job comes through.

GRIMSDYKE. The millionaire's job is, alas, no longer on. He decided to buy a couple of racehorses instead. My dear Simon—
(*he places a hand on Simon's shoulder*) at first I thought family doctoring
was not for me. Worthy work, I grant you. But not enough scope.
Not for *my* talents. How wrong I was! When you sit down and think,
it has infinite possibilities. So I'll come on the permanent staff. In
place of old Dr Cooper, now out among the kangaroos.

SIMON. But, Grim . . . (*He shakes Grimsdyke's hand warmly*) of
course, I'm delighted! After all we went right through medical
school together . . .

GRIMSDYKE. This very day I start my long career as the dear old
family doctor, who ends up having brought half the district into
the world, and pushed the other half out of it. I'm mugging up my
medicine, too. I've started on the alimentary canal. I've got as far as
the tonsils, and confidently expect to reach the appendix by Saturday.

SIMON (*enthusiastically*) We've certainly got all the facilities for an
ideal family practice—except a woman's touch.

GRIMSDYKE (*matter-of-fact*) Kind of you, old boy, but don't worry
—I can make my own arrangements in that line.

SIMON. I mean to handle the mothers and children.

GRIMSDYKE. Forgive my asking, but—(*seriously*)—how are you
off for bird?

SIMON (*with a shrug and grin*) I was advised this very morning I
ought seriously to think of marriage.

GRIMSDYKE (*shocked*) Good God! That's going a bit far to get it,
isn't it?

SIMON. Even you must admit that being hauled up the aisle is
better than being hauled before the General Medical Council.

GRIMSDYKE (*thoughtfully*) You have a point. And perhaps you're
the type. You need someone to look after you and boil your eggs
and tell you when to get your hair cut.

SIMON. But who?

GRIMSDYKE (*picking up the framed photograph of a girl from the desk*)
How about this one? She looks as if she'd do. (*Looking more closely*)
You never told me who she was.

SIMON. I expect you know her. She's Florence Nightingale.

GRIMSDYKE. Look, Simon! None of your feeble jokes, in very bad
taste . . .

SIMON. Her name really *is* Florence Nightingale. She comes from a family of long and extremely severe nursing traditions. She was a probationer on Sir Lancelot's ward, just before he retired.

GRIMSDYKE (*looks again*) Yes, I remember! She dropped a jelly in the middle of his ward-round.

SIMON (*moving up stage; solemnly*) She was my fiancée. (*He sits on the window-seat*)

GRIMSDYKE (*replacing the photograph*) Well, what are you waiting for? Drop her a postcard, ring up the Vicar, and tell him to read the banns.

SIMON. *Was*, I said. Past tense. You remember, before last Christmas, I was warded with jaundice?

GRIMSDYKE (*nodding*) A revolting sight you were, too.

SIMON. Well, Sally—that's what her friends call her—was the junior night nurse. She used to take my temperature—bring me my good night drink—lay her cool hand on my fevered brow. . . .

GRIMSDYKE (*holding up his hand*) Save your breath. You fell in love with her. (*Sadly*) All virile young patients fall in love with the junior night-nurse. (*Thoughtfully*) I think the way they rub your back with spirit has something to do with it. I hear it's how they encourage lazy bulls in the Argentine.

SIMON (*rising and taking the photograph*) Once I'd turned the right colour again—at a hospital party—last New Year's Eve—I plucked up courage at midnight and asked her to marry me.

GRIMSDYKE. And she said yes?

SIMON. I think so. You see, she had a mouthful of trifle at the time. Anyway, it made no difference. The next morning she disappeared. (*Replacing the photograph on the desk*) Just dropped her resignation in the matron's letter-box and left. Then, of course, the cat was out of the bag. *I* wasn't the only runner. There'd been a stockbroker with gall-stones. A B.B.C. chap with asthma. An airline pilot with a hernia. In the end, I decided it was some Iraq oil sheik with impacted date-stones. He was discharged the same morning. Sally simply eloped with him. I suppose she's living it up now among the camels and Cadillacs.

GRIMSDYKE. Then why hang on to her photograph? I'd have thought it better to make a wax model of the woman and stick pins in it.

SIMON (*solemnly sentimental*) Sally was the only girl I ever loved. I suppose I half-hope one day she might come back to me.

(*A telephone rings*, SIMON *answers it*)

SIMON (*into the telephone*) Dr Sparrow . . . Oh! Great heavens! The Field-Marshal. I forgot! . . . Don't . . . don't worry, Lady Forcebrace. Just keep him cool and calm—well, as cool and calm as possible. (*Putting down the telephone*) Grim, finish the surgery, will you? I've got to nip round the corner to the F.-M. (*He hastily grabs his bag and makes for the door up* L)

GRIMSDYKE. Never fear—I'm ready to cope with absolutely anything. As long as it's above the tonsil.

(WILDEWINDE *appears at the door as* SIMON *is leaving*)

WILDEWINDE. Oh, Doctor—British Railways have arrived.

SIMON. Can't stop now, Wildewinde.

(SIMON *exits*)

WILDEWINDE. Dr Grimsdyke . . .

GRIMSDYKE (*moving* R) Back in a minute, Wildewinde. Slipping up to my bedroom.

(GRIMSDYKE *snips the string round his box with a pair of scissors from the instrument tray, and leaves by the small door up* R, *box under his arm*)

WILDEWINDE (*looking round with a lost expression*) What *is* happening to the practice these days? It's a good thing poor Dr Farquarson knows nothing of it. Enough to make him perforate on the spot. (*Over his shoulder, through the door*) You'd better bring them in, I suppose.

(*A British Railways* DELIVERY MAN *appears with two large boxes tied with string, labelled in red* ACME INSTRUMENT CO.—MEDICAL SUPPLIES—URGENT *and* GLASS WITH CARE)

DELIVERY MAN. Where shall I put them?

(WILDEWINDE *silently indicates up* C *with distaste*)

(*Producing a receipt book and pencil*) Medical supplies, emergency delivery. For Dr Simon Sparrow. Can you sign?

(*With a mildly tortured expression* WILDEWINDE *signs*)

Thanks, Guv'nor. 'Fraid you'll have to give me a hand with the rest of the load.

WILDEWINDE. Dear me, dear me!

(WILDEWINDE *follows the* DELIVERY MAN *and his back is glimpsed in the doorway straining at some large, heavy and complicated load. This is completely wrapped in brown paper and labelled* ATOMIC ELECTRONICS LTD—RUSH)

DELIVERY MAN. Easy now—careful—it looks valuable.

WILDEWINDE. Have a care! I have a very delicate shoulder girdle.

(*The package is placed facing down stage beside the boxes. The* DELIVERY MAN *goes for more, leaving* WILDEWINDE *inspecting it anxiously*)

I don't know what's come over Dr Sparrow, really. He seemed so sane and normal last week.

(*The* DELIVERY MAN *reappears with two horribly contemporary chairs, and under his arm, an alarming mobile consisting of stylishly twisted wires with balls of different colours and sizes on the ends*)

DELIVERY MAN. Leave them here? (*He puts the chairs one on each side of the package*)

WILDEWINDE (*inspecting them with intense displeasure*) They seem hardly appropriate for a medical establishment.

DELIVERY MAN. No accounting for tastes, is there.

WILDEWINDE. Do people actually *sit* on those?

DELIVERY MAN. Oh, yes. I deliver a lot of them. To young married couples. Them sort of chairs, wall-to-wall carpets, colour television, and gas-fired dining candles—and you've arrived. (*Holding out the mobile*) Where shall I put this?

WILDEWINDE (*mystified*) What is it?

DELIVERY MAN. A mobile. You hangs it up. Thought very artistic.

WILDEWINDE. Think of the dusting! You'd better leave it for now. (*He indicates the window-seat*)

DELIVERY MAN. Right you are, Guv'nor. (*Looking round*) Nice set of tools the doctor's got over there. Reminds me of when I was in hospital. (*He goes to open his shirt*) Want to see the scar?

(WILDEWINDE *does not want to see the scar*)

Lovely job, hand-sewn all the way down, real embroidery. Well, so long, Guv. Got to get on with the job.

(*The* DELIVERY MAN *exits up* L)

WILDEWINDE (*remembering*) My soufflé! It will be in a state of utter collapse!

(WILDEWINDE *exits* L. *As the door shuts the smaller door* R *opens.* GRIMSDYKE *appears rather majestically. He is dressed in white trousers and a high-necked white jacket, like the doctors in American television series. Under his arm are four large smart-looking plastic notices*)

GRIMSDYKE (*his face lightening up as he spots the parcels, chairs, etc*) Good! They've arrived. (*He lays the four plastic notices on the window-seat and holds them up one by one, so that we can see them. The first says:* "X-RAY DEPARTMENT", the second "CLINICAL LABORATORY", the third "ANTENATAL CLINIC". *He discards these, though hesitating over the last one. Then he plumps for* "TO THE PSYCHIATRIST", *which he attaches by a convenient hook to the door he has just left. He next turns eagerly to the smallest of the boxes, cutting the string with scissors from his top pocket and removing the contents like a child with his Christmas stocking. Producing a large metal syringe and aiming it towards his ear*) Electric ear syringe. (*Producing a complicated stethoscope*) Fully transistorized stethoscope. (*Producing a large dial with wires; frowning*) Wonder what the hell that's for? (*Producing with particular relish a head-mirror, he straps it on and strikes a solemn pose. He continues with a thick American accent*) Don't worry, young lady. *I* will pull your little brother through. (*Holding his hands before his face*) These hands can give life! (*Winks and clicks his tongue a couple of times. His face takes on a look of alarm as a rumpus occurs off*)

SIR LANCELOT (*off*) Can't you see I've got priority? This is a surgical emergency, man!

WILDEWINDE (*off; flustered*) Perhaps if you could be a little quieter, sir, the others wouldn't hear you jump the queue?

SIR LANCELOT. How the hell can I be quiet when I'm writhing in agony? Get out of my way!

(SIR LANCELOT *enters up* L. *He is in full fishing rig, with creel and landing-net attached to his waist and rod in his hand. He is in a peculiar arched posture. His voice trails off as he takes in* GRIMSDYKE, *whose face has now reached rock bottom in alarm and despondency*)

You! Grimsdyke!

GRIMSDYKE (*after emitting croaking noises*) Er—er—an unexpected pleasure.

SIR LANCELOT. What the devil are you dressed like that for?

GRIMSDYKE (*remembering his rig*) Oh—I—er—thought it made me really look like a doctor.

SIR LANCELOT. It makes you look like a Soho male hair stylist. (*Indicating the head mirror*) Dip your headlight when you're talking to me.

(GRIMSDYKE *switches the mirror to the back of his head*)

GRIMSDYKE. I work here. (*Very timidly*) Simon Sparrow's partner.

SIR LANCELOT. And the only thing that made my retirement from St Swithin's Hospital tolerable was the thought of never again having to look at your vacuous face!

GRIMSDYKE (*overcoming his paralysis*) What are *you* doing here?

SIR LANCELOT (*thundering*) I *live* here.

(GRIMSDYKE'S *reaction to this is a look of deeper horror and a leap towards the door up* L)

GRIMSDYKE. Excuse me—I've got a case—extremely urgent . . .

SIR LANCELOT. Come back, you illegitimate descendant of Sweeny Todd!

(GRIMSDYKE *stops.* SIR LANCELOT'S *tone changes to one of menacing briskness*)

Now look here, Grimsdyke. Professionally speaking, I wouldn't trust you to worm my bitch. But I need urgent medical assistance.

GRIMSDYKE. Y-yes, sir. What's the matter?

SIR LANCELOT. Can't you see what's the matter? Lumbago, you fool! L for laryngitis, U for ulcers, M for measles, B for bronchitis, A for anthrax, G for gout, O for obesity. Lumbago!

GRIMSDYKE (*trying to recover and face the situation*) Perhaps you could manage to sit down? (*He helps Sir Lancelot into the patient's chair. Taking the rod, he props it against the huge parcel. Ingratiatingly*) Did you get any fish?

SIR LANCELOT. Of course I didn't get any fish! Do you imagine in this ridiculous posture I could hook even a plate of jellied eels? (*Merely gruff*) I'll give you the full clinical history.

GRIMSDYKE. Good, sir. (*He becomes more business-like, takes a contemporary chair, places it directly in front of Sir Lancelot and leans forward eagerly, with his hands on his knees. He switches the mirror round to the front of his head, but, remembering, immediately switches it back again)*

SIR LANCELOT (*indicating the river is near by; less fiercely*) I'd just got down to the river there.

(GRIMSDYKE *nods earnestly, and continues to do so at each new fact*)

The fish were rising everywhere. (*Motioning*) Plop, plop! All of 'em snapping like famished alligators! Then, damme! If I didn't spot dear old Horace.

GRIMSDYKE. Dear old Horace who?

SIR LANCELOT. He's a fish. The most wonderful rainbow trout in the entire river—the entire county—the entire kingdom. (*His arms extend progressively as he indicates this*) I've known him since he was a little fingerling at his mother's knee. And by jove! This morning—he took my fly!

GRIMSDYKE. Congratulations.

SIR LANCELOT. Congratulations balderdash! My nylon cast snapped, like a paper-chain. There was Horace, heading down the river like a scalded sardine. And there was I, locked in this position.

GRIMSDYKE (*after a pause*) And what do you want me to do, sir?

SIR LANCELOT. Unlock me, of course!

GRIMSDYKE (*after another pause*) That might be rather difficult.

SIR LANCELOT. Of course it isn't difficult! Any Boy Scout with a first-aid manual could show you. Lay me flat on my belly, put your knee in my back, and pull.

GRIMSDYKE (*repeating dazedly*) Put you flat on your belly—put my knee in your back—and pull. (*Hurriedly*) I'll need an assistant. (*He leaps for the intercom, and says into it*) Wildewinde! Come at once. To help with an operation.

(WILDEWINDE *enters immediately up* L, *very eager*)

WILDEWINDE. Here I am, Doctor. Have we sterilized the instruments?

GRIMSDYKE. I want you to help me put Sir Lancelot on his belly on the floor.

WILDEWINDE (*horrified*) On the floor!

GRIMSDYKE. Then put your knee in his back while I pull his shoulders.

WILDEWINDE. You're sure this operation is perfectly surgical, Doctor?

SIR LANCELOT. Get a move on! Or do you want me to die of old age first?

(WILDEWINDE *and* GRIMSDYKE, *with a good deal of struggling and complaint from* SIR LANCELOT, *get him on the floor*)

GRIMSDYKE. Come on—knees up, Mother Wildewinde.

WILDEWINDE. As you say, Doctor.

(SIR LANCELOT *yells as the treatment outlined in the dialogue foregoing is carried out. It can continue as long as needed*)

GRIMSDYKE (*brightly, as the two operators get up*) Better?

SIR LANCELOT. Now I've got indigestion as well!

WILDEWINDE. If I may make a suggestion, Doctor? When one of my ships was out East, I underwent the famous Japanese foot massage. The young person—the female young person—removed her footwear and walked (*motioning*) up and down my spine. *Very* agreeable it was, Doctor.

GRIMSDYKE. Yes, that might do the trick.

(WILDEWINDE *sits in the contemporary chair and starts taking off his boots and brightly coloured socks immediately under Sir Lancelot's nose*)

SIR LANCELOT. I will not let that filthy pair of feet contaminate *my* backbone.

WILDEWINDE. I assure you, Sir Lancelot, I'll be as gentle as a geisha girl.

GRIMSDYKE. We've got to do something, sir. I mean, we can't just have you towed away.

SIR LANCELOT. I will not . . . !

WILDEWINDE (*with boots and socks clasped delicately in one hand, prepares to start the treatment*) Where's the pain? (*He steps delicately on Sir Lancelot's back*)

SIR LANCELOT (*roars*) O-o-oh!

(SIMON *comes hastily in up* L *with his bag. He stands unseen, and amazed at the performance. Then he looks with particular puzzlement at Grimsdyke's outfit and the parcels*)

SIMON. What's going on?

GRIMSDYKE. Oh, hello, old lad. Little orthopaedic trouble.

SIR LANCELOT. Sparrow! Get me free from these ham-footed blighters at once!

(*They all raise Sir Lancelot to his feet*)

Sparrow—*you* try putting your knee in my back.

SIMON. But you might fracture something!

SIR LANCELOT. Leave *me* to do the worrying!

SIMON (*stoutly*) No, sir, I refuse, sir!

SIR LANCELOT. What? You are disobeying my orders?

SIMON (*cheerfully*) Yes. For the simple reason that *I* give the orders now. *I* am the doctor.

SIR LANCELOT (*with heavy sarcasm*) Then what do you intend, Doctor? That I go about looking like an inverted comma till my dying day?

SIMON. Wildewinde—hand me a radiology request form. And *do* put your boots on.

(WILDEWINDE *hands a coloured form from the desk, then obliges with his boots*)

I think your condition needs investigation. You ought to have an X-ray.

SIR LANCELOT. X-rays! That's all you young fellows think about these days. All at the expense of the National Health! No wonder the country's going bankrupt.

GRIMSDYKE (*picking up a six-inch needle from the instrument tray*) Do you think it would be a good idea if I tried a lumbar puncture?

SIR LANCELOT. *You* poking about in my back would have me looking like double top in the local pub dartboard.

SIMON (*firmly*) And I think we ought to have a second opinion. From a surgeon who specializes in backs. Someone like Sir Hubert Cambridge.

SIR LANCELOT. Not that feller—not if he operates in the same shocking way he plays bridge.

SIMON. Sir Lancelot, you're really not making my task any easier.

SIR LANCELOT. Oh? Giving ourselves airs and graces now, are we? When you were my student . . .

SIMON. May I point out that I am no longer?

GRIMSDYKE (*with dignity*) I associate myself with the doctor's opinion.

SIR LANCELOT (*in Grimsdyke's face*) Shut up! (*To Simon*) Now look here, young fellow-me-lad . . . (*He leans forward with quivering finger as he says this, and with a yell clutches the small of his back*)

GRIMSDYKE (*horrified*) There was a terrible snapping noise . . .

SIR LANCELOT. My braces, you fool. (*He demonstrates the severed ends. A look of delight spreads over his face as he stretches and resumes his normal posture*) Well—the physician has healed himself. Perfectly normal again. So much for your X-rays, lumbar punctures, and second opinions from second-rate surgeons.

SIMON (*puzzled*) That's very mystifying.

SIR LANCELOT. Nothing mystifying about lumbago. (*Very pleased with himself, taking his rod*) No point in hanging about this place. I'm off to tempt Horace into another indiscretion. And don't you two go round taking credit for the cure yourselves. (*To Grimsdyke*) Doubtless you are anxious to return to your toothpaste commercial. Good day.

(SIR LANCELOT *exits in a good mood*)

SIMON (*to Grimsdyke*) What's the idea of the Dr Kildare get-up?

GRIMSDYKE (*proudly*) Like it? It's quite the latest in medical styles. Long hips. I picked it up in London yesterday.

SIMON. If you want to go about like that, I suppose it's your affair. But you'll have to be jolly careful not to spill your soup. (*Turning to the packages*) And what's all this? Have they mistaken us for Bart's Hospital, or something?

WILDEWINDE. They were addressed to you, Dr Sparrow. I took the liberty of signing the man's book.

SIMON. I'll have to find who our fairy godmother was, and get him to whisk them away again. (*Briskly*) Wildewinde, tell Mrs Tadwich and the other patient we'll be ready in a second. Explain I was succouring Lord Forcebrace. (*To Grimsdyke*) Do you know, he wears medal ribbons on his pyjamas. (*To Wildewinde*) And fix me a ham sandwich or something. I've got the school clinic in half an hour.

(WILDEWINDE *leaves by the door up* L)

GRIMSDYKE (*proudly*) It was me.

(SIMON *looks lost*)

The fairy godmum. It's the new equipment I ordered yesterday in London. Let me explain. I walked into that big surgical supplies place in Wigmore Street—to buy a new stethoscope, actually. Never seemed to hear a damn thing down my old one. When suddenly—in a blinding flash—it struck me. Why should the specialist boys in hospital have all the glamour and all the chromium plate? All family doctoring needs to put it right in the clinical picture is a man of initiative—of vision—of energy—of—might we say it (*modestly*) genius? A man—like me.

SIMON. You haven't been at the purple hearts, I suppose?

GRIMSDYKE (*holding up his hand*) Let me demonstrate. Help me off with the paper, there's a good lad.

(*They rip the paper off the largest package, revealing a strange machine. Its essentials are: a slot toward the top and a chute towards the bottom, through which a strip of wide, stiffish paper can extrude from a roll; a rack of punch-cards on one side, and a metal pencil attached to the other; an illuminated panel, as yet unreadable, saying* TILT; *an ability to make a sucking noise; and an operating knob marked* PRESS. *Other decorations can be added to taste, such as lights flashing in series, rapidly revolving dials, bells and buzzers. A cable with plug trails from it*)

GRIMSDYKE. Let me proudly produce—AUTODOC. His—or her—full name is Automatic Universal Treatment or Diagnosis Office Computer—AUTODOC. Rather neat, don't you think?

SIMON. We can't have a piece of junk like that cluttering up the surgery!

GRIMSDYKE. Piece of junk! (*Taking Simon's arm and explaining kindly*) Look, Simon—we live in the computer age. Gone are the days when the doctor fumbled round just with his hands, ears, eyes and nose. Today, the marvels of modern science stand at his beck and call. We must be switched on—electronically.

SIMON. But what's it *do?*

GRIMSDYKE (*moving to a plug* R *of the window*) Everything! Let me connect it up to the mains. (*He plugs in the cable*) Now—press button A.

(SIMON *gingerly presses the button, and to his alarm the machine goes into action, with flashing lights, whirling dials, chimes, clicks. whirrs, and other effects*)

Fascinating, isn't it?

SIMON (*becoming angry*) And how many times a year do you imagine we'll want to use that fantastically complicated piece of apparatus in this fantastically *un*complicated general practice?

GRIMSDYKE. But that isn't the point! (*He operates the machine again, to Simon's added annoyance*) We just tell the patients who've nothing wrong with them—and that, you'll accept, is about half the lot— "My dear, your diagnosis is beyond the grip of mere human doctors. You need to be computerized."

SIMON (*objecting strongly*) But *that* won't do them any good!

GRIMSDYKE. I'm not with you there, Simon. They'll feel absolutely splendid after causing all that firework display. Anyway, that's all quite beside the point. Once the word gets round we've gone into partnership with AUTODOC, patients will be flocking to our list from every other doctor in the district. And we won't have to lift a finger. We switch on AUTODOC, line up the patients, and go out and play golf. Enormous success is staring us in the face. In six months I shouldn't be surprised if we didn't have to order a second one.

SIMON (*appalled*) But—but—Grim . . . (*He sees the plastic notice*) What's *that* doing on the way to your bedroom?

GRIMSDYKE (*remembering it*) Oh, that. A little bit of window-dressing. Always gives the patients confidence to think we employ a large auxiliary staff.

SIMON (*seeing the chairs*) And these—malformations!

GRIMSDYKE (*hurt*) Don't you like them? I thought they were rather stylish. I got them yesterday in the Utter Contemp. Boutique, Beauchamp Place.

SIMON (*picking up the mobile*) And this mutilated pawnbroker's sign . . .

GRIMSDYKE. My dear Simon! I know you're an excellent doctor, but you're *behind the times*. Look at this surgery—why it's like practising in the middle of the British Museum. It needs bringing up to date. Don't you read the papers? Britain today must invest in modernization.

SIMON (*angry*) How do you intend to pay for this particular investment?

GRIMSDYKE. That's no problem, I had them charge it up to the practice. You might send them a cheque some time.

SIMON. Do—do—you realize exactly how little this practice actually earns?

GRIMSDYKE. My dear fellow! You don't give me any credit for financial acumen. These things come under the heading of "legitimate practice expenses". You can knock them off your income-tax.

SIMON. Income-tax! Income-tax! Do you know how many years I'd have to work—to make enough money—to pay enough income-tax—to cover all *that*? About two and a half centuries.

GRIMSDYKE (*slightly discomforted*) Well, if you feel like that about it, I'll ring up and cancel our artificial kidney.

SIMON. You have ruined the practice not only financially, but morally. Can't you see these crackpot ideas of yours are wildly un-ethical?

(WILDEWINDE *bursts in up* L. *He has a delighted look on his face and is proudly carrying an open copy of a medical journal*)

WILDEWINDE (*moving* L *of Simon*) Oh, Dr Sparrow! Dr Sparrow! I've just seen it. Congratulations! Your name in print! And right at the top of the page, too.

SIMON. What? (*He snatches it*) In the *Medical Journal?*

GRIMSDYKE. Yes, Doctor. This morning's issue. It read *very* well. Quite a neat turn of phrase you have, if I may say so.

SIMON (*frowning deeply; reading*) "Letters to the Editor, Dear Sir, I modestly claim to have instituted an entirely new and extremely successful treatment for the very common condition of rheumatism in my practice at Hampden Cross, Hampshire. Large numbers of my patients have shown a sensational improvement after a series of injections of—*extract of seaweed.* (*He looks up in amazement, then resumes reading*) "Your obedient servant, Simon Sparrow, M.B. B.S. . . ." But I never wrote *that!* I've never written to a medical journal in my life. I . . . (*He breaks off, eyeing Grimsdyke*)

(GRIMSDYKE *looks pointedly unconcerned*)

You! (*Flourishing his journal*) You perpetrated this forgery . . .

GRIMSDYKE. Decent of them to print it, I thought. At such short notice.

SIMON. But don't you realize, you idiot, this is frank, outrageous, barefaced, bloody advertising? Do you want to get me struck off the Register, disgraced before my fellow doctors, bereft of my liveli-hood?

GRIMSDYKE (*calming him*) Calm down, calm down! I admit, Simon, that advertising *is* a sin, ethicwise. Almost as bad as adultery with your patients—though of course less fun. But certain ways—like this—you can *get away with it.*

SIMON (*hopelessly*) Seaweed injections!

GRIMSDYKE. If anyone turns up asking for them, say the seaweed is off.

WILDEWINDE (*remembering*) Injections! Oh, Dr Sparrow! That reminds me—did you find the anti-tetanus serum all right last Saturday night? I keep it in the refrigerator, under the garlic butter.

(SIMON *looks puzzled*)

I was sitting in the cinema when the slide came on. "Dr Sparrow Wanted Urgently, Case of Acute Lockjaw." Right in the middle of somebody making love to Sophia Loren.

SIMON (*rounding on Grimsdyke*) You did that!

GRIMSDYKE. I thought the lockjaw gave an arresting dramatic touch.

SIMON (*very angry*) Why don't you just buy me a spot on television?

GRIMSDYKE (*thoughtfully*) No, I think that would be going a bit far.

SIMON. You're more dangerous in medical practice than an un-labelled bottle of cyanide.

GRIMSDYKE (*offended*) No need to get personal. Ours is an old childhood friendship.

SIMON. Luckily, one of us has grown up.

GRIMSDYKE (*thoughtfully*) You know, you're developing a twisted mind.

SIMON (*loudly, pointing to the door up* L) Then why don't you go upstairs and ask the psychiatrist about it?

GRIMSDYKE (*becoming angry*) I'm not going to stand here and be insulted by a refugee from the Stone Age.

SIMON. *I'm* not stopping you!

GRIMSDYKE (*with great dignity*) I am going to my room. Kindly send Wildewinde to tell me when you have recovered your composure. (*He makes with dignity to the door up* R, *and on reaching it pauses and asks in a conversational voice*) I suppose you couldn't manage another small advance of my salary, could you?

SIMON (*loudly*) No!

(GRIMSDYKE *shrugs his shoulders and leaves.* SIMON *hurls the medical journal furiously into a corner*)

WILDEWINDE. Poor Doctor! You're upset!

SIMON (*in utter despair*) My God! (*He angrily thumps the machine, which sets into motion again*) Bah! (*He sits behind the desk and props his chin in his hand. He continues very quietly*) Wildewinde . . .

WILDEWINDE (*very solicitous*) Doctor?

SIMON. Will you please ring up an establishment called the Utter Contemp. Furnishing Boutique, in Beauchamp Place, London, and ask them to remove their—(*indicating chairs*)—merchandise.

WILDEWINDE (*surprised*) You didn't order them, Doctor?

SIMON (*resigned*) What do you imagine? And that—(*indicating the mobile*) model of a haemoglobin molecule, or whatever it is.

WILDEWINDE. Very good, Doctor. And what shall I do about the car?

SIMON (*lost*) Car?

WILDEWINDE (*becoming coy*) Yes, Doctor. It's arrived. And very stylish, I must say. The gentleman is in the waiting-room to attend to the delivery formalities. (*Handing over a visiting card from his pocket*) A Major Scruttson. Retired, I fancy.

SIMON (*reading*) "Buckingham Palace Motors, Mayfair. Specialists in Bentley and Rolls-Royce . . ."

WILDEWINDE. A very splendid one it is, too. Equipped with all etceteras, including built-in cocktail cabinet—with cocktails. (*Chidingly*) I hope you can afford it, Doctor.

SIMON (*holding his head in his hands and groaning*) I didn't order the blasted car either. Dr Grimsdyke did.

WILDEWINDE. I didn't know he was a moneyed young gentleman?

SIMON. He isn't. And neither am I. In one single afternoon I have been reduced to total bankruptcy. You can tell this major whatnot to take the car back again.

WILDEWINDE. That might be a little difficult. He seems a rather forceful gentleman.

SIMON (*banging the desk*) I don't care! (*Rising and moving up* L) Tell him to clear off. Tell him we're in quarantine—cholera—typhoid—bubonic plague—all right! *I'll* tell him.

(*As* SIMON *exits* L, GRIMSDYKE *enters* R)

GRIMSDYKE. Simon . . .

(SIMON *slams the door behind him*)

He *is* in an odd mood today. Er—Wildewinde . . .

WILDEWINDE. Doctor?

GRIMSDYKE (*moving* C) I suppose you couldn't manage another couple of quid till next Friday?

WILDEWINDE. I regret definitely not, Doctor.

GRIMSDYKE. Oh. Pity. (*Reflectively*) Remarkable the social life you can find in a sleepy little town like this.

WILDEWINDE (*superiorly, tidying up the paper round* AUTODOC) It depends what you mean by "social life". Speaking personally, I notice the lack of an art gallery.

GRIMSDYKE. Come off it, Wildewinde. I saw you in the saloon bar of the *Hat and Feathers* last Friday night. Getting as sloshed as a newt.

WILDEWINDE (*pained*) I would hardly expect such expressions to drop from the lips of a medical gentleman.

(GRIMSDYKE *laughs*)

(*Making to leave up* L) If you will pardon me, Doctor, I will go and countermand the furniture.

GRIMSDYKE. What, my Scandinavian Italian chairs? Not on your nelly! I had to sit on about fifty before picking those two. Damned uncomfortable it was.

WILDEWINDE. It happens to be Dr Sparrow's orders.

GRIMSDYKE. Is it? Well, it happens to be *my* orders you leave 'em alone.

WILDEWINDE. I do not take orders from you, Doctor.

GRIMSDYKE. Look here, you little lavender-scented hook-worm . . .

WILDEWINDE (*horrified*) Doctor!

GRIMSDYKE. If you don't behave yourself I'll tell Dr Sparrow the cause of your recurrent attacks of amnesia. That bottle of gin you keep in the back of the drug cupboard—labelled "Gripe Water".

WILDEWINDE (*alarmed*) You know my little secret!

GRIMSDYKE. *And* I'll let on about those interesting magazines which arrive for you—under plain cover.

WILDEWINDE (*horrified*) You wouldn't!

GRIMSDYKE. You might stick 'em in the waiting-room when you've finished. It would liven the place up a bit.

WILDEWINDE. I have *never* been spoken to like this in my life!

(WILDEWINDE *exits up* L *with a flourish*)

GRIMSDYKE (*disgusted*) He wouldn't even raise a couple of quid! No sense of professional solidarity.

(SIMON *enters* L, *glares at Grimsdyke, moves briskly to the desk, sits down, and starts busying himself with papers.* GRIMSDYKE *stands* C *looking into the middle distance. There is a long silence*)

Er . . .

(SIMON *glares at him.* GRIMSDYKE *notices this and coughs loudly*)

SIMON (*very briefly*) Instead of standing there, why don't you get yourself a dose of cough linctus?

GRIMSDYKE (*distantly*) I just wondered, old man, if there happened to be any cases you'd like to discuss with me.

SIMON. Yes. The last one.

GRIMSDYKE. Interesting?

SIMON. Profitable. I have just saved myself six thousand five hundred and eleven quid. And fifteen and ninepence. I cancelled the car.

GRIMSDYKE (*calmly*) You did? Rather a shame. I thought it would have lent a much-needed tone to the practice. (*Awkwardly*) Er— Simon . . .

(SIMON *says nothing*)

Hasty words were said just then. Passions were raised. Chaps became heated.

(SIMON *says nothing*)

After all, we ought to conduct ourselves with a certain dignity.

(SIMON *says nothing*)

I mean, we *are* both registered medical practitioners. The public look up to us with respect. We must set a good example.

(SIMON *still says nothing*)

I thought we should compose our differences, like doctors and gentlemen. (*He offers his hand*)

(SIMON *inspects and very briefly shakes it*)

SIMON. And now will you please go elsewhere. Anywhere elsewhere.

GRIMSDYKE (*surprised*) I thought you wanted me to finish the surgery.

SIMON. *I* am finishing the surgery. Even if I don't get to the school clinic before all the kids go home. I have decided that, for humanitarian reasons, I do not wish you to lay a finger on another of my patients.

GRIMSDYKE (*bristling*) That happens to give a very nasty impression of my professional abilities, old man.

SIMON. It does. And it's a perfectly fair impression. (*He presses the intercom*) Wildewinde, send in the next patient, please.

GRIMSDYKE (*determinedly*) You asked me to take surgery and take surgery I damn well shall!

SIMON. What the hell's wrong with you? I've never known you to meet work half-way before.

GRIMSDYKE. It happens to be a matter of principle.

SIMON. Be reasonable! We can't *both* take surgery.

GRIMSDYKE. Why not? (*He presses the intercom*) Wildewinde, send in the next *two* patients.

(GRIMSDYKE *takes the screen from up* R *and places it to divide the room into two. He takes the left section with the examination couch, and one contemporary chair.* SIMON *sits grimly at his desk, in possession of the rest of the room.* AUTODOC *continues in full view.* WILDEWINDE *ushers in* MRS TADWICH, *followed by* MR CLARIBOLD, *a youngish, nervous man with large glasses and a bowler clasped firmly in his hand. All three look confused*)

GRIMSDYKE (*spotting Mrs Tadwich*) Would you mind?

SIMON (*dully, business-like*) Mr Claribold, would you mind coming over here? I'm so sorry to have kept you waiting. This morning I've had rather a lot of difficult cases.

MR CLARIBOLD (*who has a flat, precise voice, spacing out all his phrases*) Not at all, Doctor, I realize—that your calling, has many trails and tribulations.

SIMON (*warmly*) Quite.

(MRS TADWICH *sits on the couch, showing lots of leg.* GRIMSDYKE *sits on a contemporary chair, and engages her in deep but unheard conversation.* MR CLARIBOLD *sits in the patient's chair and has great difficulty deciding what to do with his hat. He tries placing it on his knees, under the chair, behind his back.* SIMON, *meanwhile, is looking through some notes. And* WILDEWINDE, *uncertain how to cope with this highly original situation, stations himself uneasily down stage of the screen in a position of neutrality*)

SIMON. Now, Mr Claribold, what's your occupation?

MR CLARIBOLD. I am, as you might say, in the construction line, Doctor.

SIMON. You mean you're a builder?

MR CLARIBOLD. That is correct, Doctor.

SIMON (*writing*) And what's the trouble?

MR CLARIBOLD. I have, of late, suffered from severe neuralgia, in the cephalic region.

SIMON. Er—you've got headaches?

MR CLARIBOLD. That's what I said, Doctor.

SIMON. Is there any particular reason for them?

MR CLARIBOLD (*looking coy*) Well, Doctor, I think it's, er— (*hurriedly and coyly getting it out*)—sex, Doctor.

(SIMON *looks alarmed*)

You see, Doctor, I am not blessed with a lady wife. I have always left such things alone. But last month I became very interested in a certain young lady at work. I began to press my attentions on her.

SIMON (*interrupting*) Wait a minute, let me get this down. "Pressed attentions on her." Yes?

MR CLARIBOLD. But unfortunately, Doctor, she went off with a travelling gentleman from Macclesfield. I was bereft.

SIMON. I'm very sorry.

MR CLARIBOLD. Perhaps it was for the best. She had some very flighty characteristics.

SIMON. Let's get back to the headaches.

MR CLARIBOLD. It would seem this young person, aroused strange and unknown passions in me. Ever since her departure, I have had like a big weight, on the top of my cranium. I think it may be psychological, Doctor. I am all crazily mixed up inside.

SIMON. Possibly you are, but you *could* need a pair of glasses as well.

GRIMSDYKE. Wildewinde!

WILDEWINDE (*coming to him*) Doctor?

GRIMSDYKE. Will you please present Dr Grimsdyke's compliments to Dr Sparrow, and ask Dr Sparrow if he will kindly give Dr Grimsdyke Mrs Tadwich's notes.

WILDEWINDE (*crossing to Simon*) Dr Sparrow, Dr Grimsdyke presents his compliments and begs you to give him Mrs Tadwich's notes.

(*These exchanges are heard clearly by everyone in the room.* MR CLARIBOLD *looks more alarmed*)

SIMON (*handing Wildewinde a folder from his desk*) Dr Sparrow presents his compliments to Dr Grimsdyke, and what has he done with the ophthalmoscope?

WILDEWINDE (*crossing and handing the notes to Grimsdyke*) Dr Sparrow presents his compliments, and what has Dr Grimsdyke done with the ophthalmoscope?

GRIMSDYKE. Dr Grimsdyke hasn't seen the bloody ophthalmoscope. Anyway, the battery's been dead for days.

(WILDEWINDE *crosses back towards Simon*)

SIMON (*grimly*) I heard. (*He gets up and starts examining Mr Claribold's eye movements*)

GRIMSDYKE (*turning over the notes*) I'm glad to say your condition is idiopathic, Mrs Tadwich—there is nothing wrong with your heart. You can look forward to many years of happy and—(*inspecting her legs*)—active life. I don't think we shall have to see you again.

MRS TADWICH (*huskily*) But, Doctor! I'm sure I've got lots of *other* things wrong with me.

GRIMSDYKE. Good! I mean, I'm sorry.

MRS TADWICH. Shall I tell you all about my vibrations?

GRIMSDYKE. Do. (*Preparing to listen eagerly*)

MRS TADWICH. I'm really a terribly complicated person, you know.

GRIMSDYKE. Are you? (*Struck with an idea*) I'd love to have you on my computer. (*He leads her to* AUTODOC, *and hands her a card and pencil*) Just tick off your leading troubles on the card. Then the computer will tell us exactly what's wrong and how to treat it.

(MRS TADWICH *briefly ticks the card, which* GRIMSDYKE *slips into the upper slot and presses the button. The machine goes into action, and a foot or so of printed paper extrudes from the lower chute, which he inspects. He looks up at Mrs Tadwich and whistles*)

I *say!*

(*The machine continues*)

I think I ought to sedate you.

(SIMON *moves to the machine and gives it an enormous shove. It stops, and a panel lights up to indicate* TILT. SIMON *stands face to face with* GRIMSDYKE)

Dr Grimsdyke presents his compliments to Dr Sparrow and would like the butobarbitone tablets.

SIMON (*briefly*) Dr Sparrow has finished the bottle.

GRIMSDYKE. What, all of it? What have you been doing? Doping racehorses?

WILDEWINDE (*horrified by the turn of events*) Doctor, doctors, really! Not in front of the patients.

SIMON (*sternly indicating the door up* L) Wildewinde—leave the room.

WILDEWINDE (*highly annoyed*) Very well, Doctor.

(WILDEWINDE *exits up* L)

GRIMSDYKE. I'll have to write a prescription, then. (*Having produced a prescription pad and pencil from his pocket, he chews the pencil thoughtfully*) Will Dr Sparrow kindly refresh Dr Grimsdyke's memory on the dose of butobarbitone?

SIMON. Two hundred milligrams.

GRIMSDYKE (*considering this*) No, it isn't. It's five hundred milligrams.

SIMON (*crossly*) It's *two* hundred milligrams.

GRIMSDYKE (*coming close and wagging a finger*) I tell you, it's *five* hundred milligrams.

(*They circle round as they argue*)

SIMON. It's *not* five hundred milligrams! It's *two* hundred milligrams.

GRIMSDYKE. I distinctly remember learning in my pharmacology classes that the dose of butobarbitone is—(*shouting*)—*five hundred milligrams.*

SIMON. You are completely mistaken because it's—(*shouting*)—*two hundred milligrams.*

(*They starts giving each other pushes to emphasize their points*)

GRIMSDYKE. It's five!
SIMON. It's two!
GRIMSDYKE. *Five!*
SIMON. *Two!!*

(*They start jostling in earnest*)

MR CLARIBOLD (*jumping up and clasping his head*) Oh! My headache!

(*The* DELIVERY MAN *enters by the door up* L, *nonchalantly removes the two contemporary chairs, and leaves*)

I do hope they don't hurt each other. I faint directly, at the sight of blood.

MRS TADWICH. Don't worry. I'm good at first aid. . . . It's in my horoscope.

SIMON. Take your hand off me!
GRIMSDYKE. Get off my foot!
SIMON. You're fired.
GRIMSDYKE. Impossible. I've just resigned. (*He grabs his ridiculous hat and puts it on. With great dignity*) I shall take up temporary residence at the *Hat and Feathers*. A man will call for my things.

(WILDEWINDE *bursts in up* L *with another of the plastic notices*)

WILDEWINDE (*furious*) Dr Sparrow! I am leaving this very instant! I have never been so insulted in all my born days. *Look* what I found on my bedroom door! (*He holds up the notice which we see announces* FAMILY PLANNING CONSULTANT)

GRIMSDYKE (*hustling Wildewinde out*) You can buy the first pint.

(WILDEWINDE *exits up* L, *followed by* GRIMSDYKE)

SIMON. I'm afraid Dr Grimsdyke has had a lot of trouble with his nerves recently. Overwork. A very brilliant man, you know. These geniuses are sometimes a little eccentric.

MRS TADWICH. I *quite* understand, Doctor. He vibrates, too. (*To Mr Claribold*) Perhaps it would be simpler if you just went down to the chemist for an aspirin?

(*With a little smile* MRS TADWICH *leads* MR CLARIBOLD *out* L. SIMON *gives a sigh and kneels to pick up and study the strip of paper from* AUTODOC. *He finds himself eyeing a very shapely pair of girl's legs, and quite a lot of them, too. These belong to* KITTEN, *who has come in quietly by the door up* L. *She is very young, very pretty, and very brainless. She is dressed in the latest of teenage fashion, and carries a small suitcase. She has the fashionable deadpan teenage manner*)

SIMON (*in quiet resigned amazement*) Who are you?
KITTEN. I'm Kitten. (*She puts her case down by the door*)
SIMON (*frowning in deep perplexity*) What do you want?

KITTEN. I've come to see the doctor.

SIMON (*rising*) I'm the doctor. (*He crosses* R *to the dressing-bin and drops the paper inside*)

KITTEN. No, the other doctor. The one with the kind blue eyes.

SIMON (*wearily*) I'm afraid Dr Grimsdyke has been called to a very difficult case. It is very unlikely that he himself will ever recover from it.

KITTEN (*disappointed*) Oh!

SIMON (*sitting behind the desk*) Well, Miss . . . ?

KITTEN. Strudwick. (*After a pause*) But all my friends call me Kitten.

SIMON. If you'll kindly sit down and tell me what's the matter, I'll do my best for you.

KITTEN. Ta. (*She sits pertly on the patient's chair*) But nothing's the matter with me. (*She giggles*) At least, I hope not.

SIMON. Then what do you want to see the doctor for?

KITTEN. I've come to start the job. Nurse-receptionist. Dr Grimsdyke gave it to me last night. (*Handing over a National Insurance Card*) There's my card. It's stamped up to date.

SIMON (*staring at her*) Have you had much experience in the nursing profession?

KITTEN. Oh, no. But I'll be all right. I can turn my hand to anything. My mum always says so.

SIMON. Then what *have* you had experience of?

KITTEN. In Jennifer Modes, Oxford Street. I was window-dressing.

SIMON. I bet you were.

KITTEN. I didn't care for it much. Those men! How they used to stare! You were thankful you had a dirty great sheet of plate glass between you and them sometimes.

SIMON. And was that—if I may ask—how you met Dr Grimsdyke?

KITTEN. It was at the ten-pin bowling. (*She simpers*) I could tell he was a doctor from the start. He had such dreamy soft hands. (*She pauses*)

(SIMON *stares at her*)

Well, where's my room? He said it was a residential job. He wanted to have me handy in case of emergency during the night.

SIMON (*covering his face in his hands*) Miss Strudwick—Kitten . . . (*He uncovers his face and looks at her again, a thought striking him as he asks briskly*) Can you cook? Nothing elaborate—bacon and eggs, fish and chips, Sunday roast?

KITTEN. I've cooked for my dad, and he's hard enough to please, I'm telling you.

SIMON (*getting up and starting to walk about, eagerly*) You can answer the telephone? You can write a message? And I'm sure at Jennifer Modes you were awfully good in handling talkative and sometimes difficult middle-aged women? *And* helping them in and out of their clothes?

(KITTEN *nods with increasing assertion to all this*)

Right, Kitten, you're on the strength. Here's the official overall.

(SIMON *tosses her a folded white overall from the shelf with the sterilizer.* KITTEN *rises and puts it on, carefully hitching up the skirt about a foot and a half until it is on the level of her own very short one*)

(*Moving to her down* C) I hope you will find the work both interesting and rewarding. There's a very comfortable bed-sitting-room beside the kitchen, recently vacated by your predecessor. Very recently.

KITTEN (*admiring the effect of her costume*) What fab. gear! (*Struck by a thought, and looking doubtful*) Are you married?

SIMON (*lightly*) I'm not actually.

KITTEN (*looking wary*) Oh!

SIMON. You mean—but another doctor's moving in this very day to replace Dr Grimsdyke. He's Dr Nicholas Barrington, and I hope you're going to like him.

KITTEN. I'm sure I will. I like all doctors.

SIMON. He's probably got dreamy soft hands, too. So you see you're just as safe as if you had—a dirty great sheet of plate-glass between us. You'll soon find your way round.

KITTEN (*pointing to the sterilizer*) What's that?

SIMON. With that we achieve sterility.

KITTEN. The things they can do with you these days!

SIMON (*picking up her hands and inspecting them*) These finger-nails, though a beautiful violet hue, must, I fear, be reduced to something under three inches.

KITTEN. If I'm going to be a nurse, I'd better look the part, hadn't I? (*Giggles*) You're rather nice, too.

SIMON (*dropping her hands*) Quite. Well . . .

(*The telephone rings*)

(*Moving above the desk and picking up the receiver; to Kitten*) Be a dear and go to the kitchen and fix me a sandwich—(*indicating the door* L)—second door on the right through there.

(KITTEN, *taking her suitcase, exits* L)

(*Into the telephone*) Dr Sparrow . . . Who? Oh, yes, Mrs Whitaker . . . Your young Johnnie . . . Fell out of a tree. What, again? . . . H'm . . . H'm . . . Of course it *might* be a fracture. These children's bones bend very easily . . . All right, I'll come straight round. Don't worry. Just lay him down and cheer him up. (*He puts down the receiver, picks up his bag from below the sterilizer, and hastily crams in some dressings*)

(*There is a knock on the door up* L)

Come in. (*He continues his activities with the bag, his back to the door*)

(NIKKI *enters. She is very pretty and charming, and faces life with perfect confidence. She is dressed smartly, but not flamboyantly*)

NIKKI (*after a pause*) Dr Sparrow?

SIMON (*in surprise, turning and gathering up his bag, clearly not disposed to waste time with the interloper*) Yes, that's right. But I can't see you now, I'm afraid, I've been called to a case. If you wander out the way you wandered in you'll find a receptionist somewhere, she'll give you an appointment.

NIKKI. I'm not a patient. I came about the job.

SIMON (*briefly, starting towards the door up* L) It's gone.

NIKKI (*surprised*) Already?

SIMON (*explaining for dimwits*) The vacancy has just been filled.

NIKKI. That's a disappointment. I was led to believe I could simply walk into it.

SIMON (*briefly and unsympathetically*) I expect a lot of other girls were led to believe they could simply walk into it, too.

NIKKI (*frowning, mildly complaining*) I came down here as soon as I possibly could.

SIMON. The earlier bird got the worm. (*Moving to the desk*) Perhaps you shouldn't keep so many late nights. (*He flicks the intercom*)

NIKKI (*mystified*) I don't think I do, particularly.

SIMON (*into the intercom*) Kitten? Can you hear me? Good. I've got to dash out and see a patient. This new doctor may arrive while I'm away. Fix him up with a cup of tea or a glass of beer. (*Reflecting*) I hope the bastard drinks beer! Ask him to dump his gear in the pink bedroom. That's the one next to mine. Warn him when it rains there's a waterfall through the roof. If he objects I won't mind if he moves in with me till we get the builders in. As long as he doesn't snore. Got all that? Fine. I'm sure I can trust you to entertain him till I get back. (*Making towards the door up* L; *over his shoulder to Nikki*) I'm sorry, but I'm afraid there's absolutely no point in your hanging about any longer.

NIKKI (*rather resentful*) I wish I had known earlier, Dr Sparrow. It would at least have saved me a very tedious journey from Town.

SIMON (*becoming exasperated*) Don't blame *me! I* can't help it if he's offering the job to half the girls in London.

NIKKI (*lost, smiling incredulously*) Who are you talking about?

SIMON. Grimsdyke. Dr Grimsdyke. Him of the dreamy hands. I suppose you realize you are keeping me from treating a poor sick child, who has just dropped out of an apple tree, and is lying screaming in his mother's arms, with a horribly mangled right leg?

NIKKI. That'll probably be a greenstick fracture.

SIMON (*unthinkingly*) Yes, it probably *is* a greenstick.

NIKKI. Well, with proper immobilization under X-ray check it'll unite in about three weeks. As long as the vascular supply hasn't been interfered with, of course. You can have the child weight-bearing in a matter of days, so it shouldn't be too disastrous.

SIMON (*dropping his bag and staring at her in horror*) You—you're . . .

NIKKI (*matter-of-fact*) Dr Barrington. Dr Nichola Barrington.

SIMON (*moving to the desk*) But—but—(*he snatches up the letter from the desk*)—you ought to be—I thought you were—Dr *Nicholas* Barrington.

NIKKI (*smiling*) That's a mistake that's always happening. When I was a student I was always being put down to play in the rugger fifteen.

SIMON (*totally demoralized, letting the letter flutter to the ground*) Erk—ahh—ummmm . . .

NIKKI (*very pleasantly*) I do hope it doesn't embarrass you?

SIMON. Gurrk—erruck—what have I done? (*Noticing the intercom*) What have I *said*? The pink bedroom! And I thought you were one of my former partner's little tarts—I mean . . .

NIKKI. Do I take it the job's still going?

SIMON. Yes, indeed! (*Looking round wildly*) Won't you have some lunch?

NIKKI. I've had it, thanks.

SIMON. Or a drink?

NIKKI. Not in the daytime.

SIMON. Cup of tea?

NIKKI. Perhaps later.

SIMON (*becoming desperate*) A chair?

NIKKI. Thank you. (*She sits on the patient's chair*)

SIMON. I don't know how to apologize. If you're not going to walk out on the spot, as you've every right to . . .

NIKKI. But I'm dying to take the job—if you'll have me.

(KITTEN *bursts in* L *with a plate containing a ham sandwich, and pulls up short*)

SIMON. Our nurse. She's new. Brand new. Miss—er Kitten. (*To Kitten*) *This* is Dr Barrington.

KITTEN (*moving above Nikki to Simon at the desk*) A change of sex? Here's your sandwich.

SIMON (*taking the sandwich and biting it; to Nikki*) Would you excuse me? Rushed morning.

(KITTEN *moves to the door up* L)

NIKKI. You look as though I ought to start work at once.

SIMON (*eagerly*) Could you? I've got to cope with this fracture.

NIKKI (*rising*) Though I'd like to get to my room and change. I only put this outfit on to impress you.

SIMON (*flattered*) Did you?

NIKKI. I thought you were going to be a terribly overwhelming old man.

SIMON (*discomforted*) Kitten, show Dr Barrington to the pink bedroom. And ring up a builder—Mr Claribold will do. (*To Nikki*) I'll be back as soon as I can.

NIKKI (*moving to the door up* L; *smiling*) By the way—I bet you half a crown that *is* a greenstick fracture.

SIMON (*standing looking dazedly after them*) What a fool I was? *Nichola Barrington!* (*His face and tone take on a pleasantly speculative tone*) Nichola Barrington? (*More gaily and loudly as he grabs his bag and trips towards the door up* L) Nichola Barrington!

SIMON *exits* L, *but immediately he reopens the door and dashes across to the desk. He grabs the photograph of Florence Nightingale, stares round wildly for somewhere to hide it, and finally drops it firmly in the dressing-bucket. With a smug look on his face he trips gaily out again, as—*

the CURTAIN *falls*

ACT II

SCENE—*The same. A fortnight later, one o'clock in the morning.*
The room has been restored to its appearance at the start of Act I, except that the AUTODOC *is still in place up* C, *the curtains closed across the window, and a large, pretty vase of flowers stands on the desk.*

When the CURTAIN *rises the room is in darkness. Immediately* NIKKI *enters* L, *switching on the lights.* SIMON *follows. They have just come home from an enjoyable evening out.* NIKKI *moves* C *and sits on the patient's chair.*

NIKKI. That was a marvellous dinner! I don't know when I've tasted such a lovely steak.

SIMON (*crossing above Nikki to the desk*) I have a certain influence in the Country Club kitchens. The chef's been a patient of the practice for years—chronic dyspepsia.

NIKKI. I'd no idea such a gay place existed out in the country.

SIMON (*sitting on the downstage edge of the desk*) We're in the middle of the stockbroker belt now, you know. And by the way—I bet you do the shake better than any other member of the medical profession.

NIKKI (*laughing*) You're not so bad yourself. It was fun, wasn't it?

SIMON. Except for one thing that completely ruined my evening.

(NIKKI *looks puzzled*)

Your total and unyielding insistence that *you* paid half the bill.

NIKKI (*chiding*) You know what I explained before we left.

SIMON. But I *did* ask you out.

NIKKI. You said you wanted to discuss the patients—quietly, away from the telephone. You never told me there was going to be a band.

SIMON. I suppose I didn't think you'd have come otherwise.

NIKKI. Now, Simon—(*trying to be firm, despite herself*)—remember our relationship is a strictly professional one.

(SIMON *nods with sad resignation*)

(*She explains with emphasis*) We're just two doctors working together in the National Health Service. Like thousands of others. The fact that one of us happens to be female is really quite irrelevant.

SIMON (*looking at her blankly*) Is it?

NIKKI (*smiling*) Anyway, I let you pay *all* the tip.

SIMON (*rising and moving* R) But, Nikki! That ulcer of Dr Farquarson's is improving every day. I'm terribly afraid he's soon going to be better. Then he'll be back at work. Then you'll simply disappear.

(*Struck with an idea*) Why not come in with us permanently? In place of Dr Cooper, out in Australia. I'm sure we'd get on splendidly. (*Quickly*) Professionally, of course.

NIKKI. It's a kind offer, Simon. And I'm flattered. You know how I enjoy this family doctoring—but you also know how I definitely intend to specialize. Anyway, perhaps your Dr Grimsdyke will turn up again.

SIMON (*moving behind the desk; concerned*) I wish I knew where he'd got to. I've searched every pub in the district. And you know this postcard I got. (*Picking a postcard from the desk and reading*) "Please send fruit cake to await collection Foulness post office, enclosing hacksaw." I'm afraid something—unmentionable might have happened to the poor fellow. (*He sits and dials*)

NIKKI (*indicating* AUTODOC) And they're calling to take away his friend tomorrow.

SIMON (*on the telephone*) Hampden Cross 3128 here. You can stop transferring our calls, thank you. (*He puts down the telephone and manipulates a switch in its base*) I've put through the extension bell to Kitten's room. Now, *Wildewinde* would never answer it at night.

NIKKI. Tell me, Simon, was Wildewinde a secret drinker.

SIMON (*rising*) I think he was a secret everything.

NIKKI (*rising*) Well—I must go to bed.

(*There is a pause*)

SIMON. Er—yes, I must go to bed, too.

(*Another pause, in which they look at each other rather awkwardly*)

NIKKI. Good night, Simon.
SIMON. Good night, Nikki.

(*Neither move*)

NIKKI (*moving up* C; *making herself more firm*) Good *night*, Simon!
SIMON (*hopelessly*) Good night, Nikki. (*He opens the small door* R, *politely*)

NIKKI. I'll use the *front* stairs, thank you, Simon.
SIMON. *What* did you say you were going to specialize in?
NIKKI (*moving up* L) Child psychology. Nightie-night.

(SIMON *exits* R, NIKKI L. *The stage is empty for a moment. Then* GRIMSDYKE'S *head pops through the window curtains, looking round wildly*)

GRIMSDYKE. No-one about. (*Behind him*) Come on—make an effort.

WILDEWINDE (*off; pathetically*) I'm stuck.

GRIMSDYKE. You ought to have gone on a diet ages ago. Grab my hand.

WILDEWINDE (*off*) Oh, Doctor! It's catching my xiphisternum.

GRIMSDYKE. Damn your xiphisternum! Mind my cuff-links.

(GRIMSDYKE *and* WILDEWINDE *fall into the room. Both are dressed in normal clothes.* GRIMSDYKE *carries a duffle bag and* WILDEWINDE *an attache-case*)

Shhh! If only I hadn't had the decency to post my key back, we'd have been spared the indignity of behaving like a couple of out-of-work burglars.

WILDEWINDE (*pathetically*) You could have rung the front-door bell.

GRIMSDYKE (*moving* LC) Use your loaf. When you want your old job back, you don't knock up the boss at one in the morning and ask for it.

WILDEWINDE (*admiringly*) Of course, Doctor. You have a mind that thinks of every detail. I don't know where we would have been without it during our recent period of incarceration. (*He sneezes*)

GRIMSDYKE. Shhh! For God's sake!

WILDEWINDE. I'm sorry. But you know what to expect after being in *that* awful place.

GRIMSDYKE. I suppose you slept with your cell door open? (*Looking round*) I could do with a drink.

WILDEWINDE (*proudly*) If you will permit me, Doctor, I think I can supply your every need. (*He goes eagerly to the cupboard and rummages inside, then turns with a look of horror*) It's gone.

GRIMSDYKE (*casually*) Try the other one you hid behind Gray's *Anatomy*. (*He idly presses the button of* AUTODOC, *which flashes and produces a tongue of paper, waving at him. He reaches for it, and it immediately disappears with a loud sucking noise. He shrugs his shoulders*)

WILDEWINDE (*moving a heavy book*) I fear Dr Sparrow has tumbled to my little failing. (*He leaves the cupboard door open*)

GRIMSDYKE (*not much concerned with Wildewinde's tragedies*) I don't know about you, but after a fortnight on a hard bed, all I'm looking forward to is a decent night's sleep.

WILDEWINDE (*moving up* L) All *I'm* looking forward to is—(*coyly*)—a poached egg on toast. The cuisine was *very* indifferent.

GRIMSDYKE. What do you expect from the Foulness Cold Cure Research Hospital? We didn't go there for our health. (*Taking his bag and making for the door up* R) You can mess about in the kitchen all night, as far as I'm concerned. I'm off to my room. I'll sort everything out with Dr Sparrow in the morning. (*He pauses in the doorway*) Wait a minute—there was a new doctor coming. A bloke called Barry—Berry—I dunno. If I find him installed, he'll just have to move over. Night, Wildewinde.

(GRIMSDYKE *exits* R)

WILDEWINDE. Good night, Doctor. (*He gives an enormous sneeze*) Bless me!

(WILDEWINDE *exits up* L. *The room is empty for a minute, then* NIKKI *enters up* L *in a nightie and dressing-gown*)

NIKKI. I *knew* I'd left the lights on. (*She pauses with her hand on the switch, noticing the cupboard has been left open. She crosses to it, and picks up the heavy book. She locks the cupboard and takes the book*) Gray's *Anatomy.* (*Moving up* L) That might do the trick.

(SIMON *enters* R *in pyjamas and dressing-gown.* NIKKI *jumps*)

SIMON. Oh—hello, Nikki.
NIKKI (*at a loss*) Hello.
SIMON. Are you getting a cold?
NIKKI. I—I don't think so.
SIMON. Funny. I thought I heard you sneeze.
NIKKI. No—I—don't think I've sneezed since last Christmas.
SIMON. I must have been dreaming. What on earth are you doing with Gray's *Anatomy?*
NIKKI. I couldn't sleep. I thought I'd come down and get some terribly heavy textbook. That might send me off.
SIMON (*brightly*) I can't sleep, either.
NIKKI. I thought you said you were dreaming?
SIMON (*put out*) Well, sort of day-dreaming.
NIKKI. I see.

(*There is a pause*)

SIMON. Good night, Nikki.
NIKKI. Good—good night, Simon.

(SIMON *disappears through the door* R, *but reappears at once*)

SIMON. Do you think I ought to take a sleeping-pill?
NIKKI (*laughing*) Well, you're the doctor.
SIMON. I believe they're habit-forming. Or are they? Perhaps *one* wouldn't matter. Shall I take butobarbitone or sodium amytal? I've never had insomnia before.
NIKKI. Neither have I. (*Quickly*) It often happens with a change of environment, doesn't it?
SIMON (*doubtfully*) Perhaps I'll just try counting sheep.

(*There is a pause, and* SIMON *leaves again. This time they merely nod at each other, feeling the words "Good night" can be left unsaid. At once* SIMON *reappears*)

I think I'll have a hot drink instead.
NIKKI. At this rate it'll soon be time for your early-morning tea.
SIMON (*grabbing an X-ray from the desk*) Mrs Tadwich's new X-rays. Will you give me a second opinion on them?
NIKKI. What, at this hour of the night?
SIMON. Yes. Now. You see, I won't have a chance to discuss them before surgery tomorrow morning.
NIKKI (*glad of the excuse*) Of course, if it's a matter of duty towards the patients . . .

(SIMON *brings her to the centre of the room, and holding the X-ray to the light with her close beside him*)

SIMON. Definitely. To a good doctor the patients always come first. Anything abnormal?

NIKKI. The diaphragm's a little high on the right.

SIMON. But the—(*dropping the X-ray down on the desk and looking at her meaningfully*)—heart's in the right place.

NIKKI (*catching on*) Yes, I—think the heart's in the right place.

SIMON (*quickly*) Did you read that paper in the *Lancet* this week? About genes? Funny to think all over the world people are going about with bunches of thousands and thousands of little genes, looking for other bunches of thousands and thousands of little genes. Just to make bunches of thousands and thousands of other little genes.

NIKKI (*quietly*) Heredity is very interesting.

SIMON (*looking into her eyes, rather breathlessly*) Nikki, I think you've got the most beautiful genes in the entire evolutionary scale. Oh, I know plenty of lady doctors are charmers, but there's an awful lot with legs like a billiard-table, and the personality of a bulldozer. But you, Nikki! (*Bursting out and jumping about*) You're wonderful! And I love you. (*Beating his torso*) With every bit of my anatomy and physiology and psychology. (*Loudly*) I love you!

NIKKI (*alarmed*) Simon, you mustn't get excited . . .

SIMON. But I *want* to get excited! This is the most exciting thing that's ever happened to me. Even more than when I got through my finals after making an awful bosh of the clinical.

NIKKI (*moving away down* LC; *all tortured*) Simon, I'm terribly fond of you, but we *can't* get involved in a love affair.

SIMON (*following her*) Why ever not? I can't think of two nicer people.

NIKKI. But I've got a career . . .

SIMON. We can have dozens of our own children to practise your psychology on.

NIKKI (*being firm with herself*) We mustn't get involved *emotionally*. I told myself that when I arrived. It wouldn't be fair on the patients.

SIMON (*moving up* c) Oh, to hell with the bloody patients.

NIKKI. It wouldn't be fair on us. We've only known each other a fortnight. No, Simon. We must remain partners at the bedside—no further.

SIMON (*disconsolately*) We don't seem to be only in the middle of the stockbroker belt. We seem to be in the middle of the chastity belt.

NIKKI (*moving to Simon up* c) Poor Simon! I suppose I'm just a pig-headed little girl underneath. (*She kisses him somewhat chastely*) Good night.

SIMON (*making resignedly for the door up* R) Good night. By the way, those weren't Mrs Tadwich's X-rays. They were the Vicar's.

(SIMON *exits up* R. NIKKI *stands looking after him with a confused expression. The telephone rings, but she picks it up at once, and sits at the desk*)

NIKKI (*into the telephone*) Dr Barrington here . . . Yes, Mrs Stewart . . . I shouldn't worry, babies swallow all sorts of things . . . I suppose it will be awkward, your husband going to the office without any collar-studs. I'm afraid the only thing I can suggest is a sports shirt. Good night. (*She puts down the telephone*)

(KITTEN *comes running in up* L, *wearing only a shortie nightie and high-heeled slippers with enormous pom-poms*)

Sorry, Kitten, the phone got you out of bed. I was here, so I answered it.

KITTEN. That's all right. (*After a pause*) Can't you sleep?

NIKKI (*hastily*) I suffer badly from insomnia. Since childhood. I'm a martyr to it.

KITTEN. Go on. It's him, isn't it? Dr Sparrow.

NIKKI (*smiling, but embarrassed*) Really, Kitten! As far as I'm concerned he's—another medical practitioner.

KITTEN (*sitting on the upstage end of the desk*) Never did I think that I would have to give advice to a highly-qualified lady. You love him, dear, don't you?

NIKKI. Of course not!

KITTEN. It's all over you! Like that nasty rash on the little girl Mrs Pickles brought in this afternoon. And as for Dr Sparrow! Coo! (*Shaking her head sadly*) The suffering! Fair makes your heart bleed to watch, it does.

NIKKI (*rising; confessing*) I *am* fond of Dr. Sparrow. And he *is* fond of me. But I don't think there's anything we can do about it.

KITTEN (*incredulous*) Nothing you can do about it? Don't you read *Honey?*

NIKKI (*moving up* L) It's kind of you to take such interest in the case, but . . . I'm afraid there's no hope of a cure.

(NIKKI *exits* L)

KITTEN. Nut cases, the pair of them, if you ask me. (*Moving above the desk*) Nothing they can do about it! They ought to try a bit of window-dressing in Oxford Street. *That* would teach them about life.

(NIKKI *enters* L *hurriedly, looking worried*)

NIKKI. Kitten . . . (*She sits down in the patient's chair, facing down stage. She swallows several times before she is able to say in a strained voice*) There's a man asleep in my bed.

KITTEN (*enthusiastically*) What's he like?

NIKKI. Horrible! (*She covers her face in her hands*) Simply horrible. Quite young, but a terribly depraved face. He's lying there on his back with his mouth wide open—snoring.

KITTEN (*leaping for the telephone*) I'll get the police.

NIKKI. No, don't do that . . .

KITTEN. Yes, I will. There's a lot of assaulting going on these days. You've only got to read the papers.

NIKKI (*rising and preventing her from lifting the phone*) We don't want a lot of great policemen tramping round the place at this hour. I'm sure we can get rid of him ourselves. I must wake up Dr Sparrow. Or rather, *we* must wake up Dr Sparrow.

KITTEN. Okay. (*She moves up* R)

(NIKKI *indicates the briefness of Kitten's costume.* KITTEN *pulls out the skirt*)

Nice, isn't it? C. and A. Very reasonable.

NIKKI. I think a dressing-gown . . .

KITTEN. Haven't got a dressing-gown. (*She thinks for a second, her finger at her open mouth*) I'll wear my transparent mac.

(KITTEN *runs across* L *and exits.* NIKKI *stands casting anxious glances upstairs* L. KITTEN *reappears, still in her nightie, in a state of speechlessness*)

(*Sitting in the same position as Nikki adopted, and staring straight ahead*) There's one in mine, too.

NIKKI. A man?

KITTEN (*nodding vigorously*) A *horrible* old man! Oooo! All flabby.

NIKKI. What on earth's going on? Have all the local vagrants mistaken us for the Salvation Army? Or is there an epidemic of male sleep-walking?

KITTEN (*still alarmed*) Very prone to that, males are.

NIKKI (*moving up* L) I'll go and see for myself.

KITTEN (*rising and grabbing Nikki's* R *arm*) No, no, don't! He's a real interferer of women. You can tell by his face.

NIKKI. We'll get Dr Sparrow, then.

KITTEN. I will *not* leave this room! Not on any account! Why, we've got sex maniacs like mice.

(WILDEWINDE, *in very gaudy pyjamas and his short white jacket, appears at the door* L *and sneezes.* KITTEN *screams and clutches* NIKKI *as they back away up* R)

WILDEWINDE (*haughty*) Who might you girls be?

NIKKI. And who might *you* be?

WILDEWINDE. *I* am Dr Sparrow's right hand.

KITTEN (*pointing accusingly*) I thought you'd been fired!

WILDEWINDE (*outraged*) I was merely taking a little holiday. Well deserved.

KITTEN. You can take another one. *I* am now Dr Sparrow's right hand.

WILDEWINDE (*more outraged*) You! In *that?*

NIKKI (*moving* C *and taking charge, briskly*) She wears something else in the surgery. We can sort out who's got the job in the morning.

WILDEWINDE. Would you oblige me by belting up, whoever you are?

NIKKI (*matter-of-fact*) I'm Dr Barrington . . .

WILDEWINDE (*overcome*) Oh—er—Doctor—that—(*bowing low*)— was only a manner of speaking, Doctor. Welcome, Doctor, to the practice. It will be a pleasure to serve a professional lady. I hope you will find my cooking agreeable—I make a teeny speciality of soufflé—and that your room's quite comf . . . (*A look of horror comes over his face as he looks hopelessly upwards*)

NIKKI (*resignedly, pointing upwards*) Who is it?

WILDEWINDE. Dr Grimsdyke.

(KITTEN *screams loudly and goes into hysterics*)

NIKKI (*coping with this*) Come along, Mr Wildewinde. We'd better lay her on her bed. The one you've just got out of.

WILDEWINDE. Oh, dear! (*Coy giggle*) I *thought* it was nice and warm.

NIKKI (*helping Kitten towards the door* L) Bring the amytal, will you? It's in the drug cupboard, where your bottle of gin was.

(NIKKI *leaves with* KITTEN, *leaving* WILDEWINDE *looking abashed. As he takes the bottle from the cupboard* R GRIMSDYKE *enters from the door up* R. *He is in pyjamas and wearing a dirty raincoat instead of a dressing-gown*)

GRIMSDYKE (*moving* RC; *crossly*) What the hell are you doing down here?

WILDEWINDE. Oh! Doctor . . . (*He starts backing away below Grimsdyke across the room, giving an awkward grin and waving the bottle of pills at him*) I—I—emergency, Doctor! (*He sneezes*)

GRIMSDYKE (*moving* C) Look here, you little septic love-bite . . .

(WILDEWINDE *shoots out of the door* L *and* SIMON, *looking confused, enters* R. *His face lights up as he sees Grimsdyke*)

SIMON. Grim! It was *you*! By God, it's good to see you back.

GRIMSDYKE (*cheering up*) Simon!

SIMON (*a look of horror coming over his face*) But you've been in . . . ?

GRIMSDYKE (*sombrely*) The place from which I was released early this morning *was* a little embarrassing. Particularly with Wildewinde.

SIMON (*more horrified*) With *Wildewinde?* Oh! The shame I've inflicted on you.

GRIMSDYKE. It was a bit infra dig, I admit.

SIMON (*very contrite*) It's all my fault. Because I was a bit hasty, I led you to do something rash and foolish . . . How can you ever forgive me?

GRIMSDYKE (*airily*) One is big enough to overlook these things. I get the job again, of course?

SIMON. Of course! With back pay. (*Very concerned*) But this will get to the ears of the General Medical Council.

GRIMSDYKE (*puzzled*) What will?

SIMON. What—whatever you did with Wildewinde.

GRIMSDYKE. There's nothing actually unethical about being a guinea-pig in the Foulness Cold Research place. Mind, I wouldn't recommend it. They stuffed cold virus up my snout every afternoon and hosed me down with ice-cold water. Brrrrr! But it provided free board and lodging and complete isolation, especially from my creditors.

SIMON. I thought you were in jail!

GRIMSDYKE (*offended*) What on earth put *that* in your head. (*Yawning and making for the door* R) Now I *must* get some sleep. I hope you had that broken guttering repaired in my room while I was away?

SIMON. Wait!

GRIMSDYKE (*surprised*) What's the matter?

SIMON. Your room. There's someone in it.

GRIMSDYKE. Well, there wasn't a moment ago.

SIMON. You mustn't go back!

GRIMSDYKE (*returning to Simon* C) That's a nice thing to tell me when I'm dressed like this.

SIMON. I'll explain. You remember before you left, I was getting another temporary locum?

GRIMSDYKE. Fellow called Bertram, or something.

SIMON. Barrington. A Dr Barrington.

GRIMSDYKE. That's right. What's he like? One of the boys or a bit of a toffee-nosed stick-in-the-mud? Lot of them about these days.

SIMON (*awkwardly*) No—he's er—very pleasant.

GRIMSDYKE. That's a blessing.

SIMON. In fact he's—very nice indeed. A very charming, agreeable personality. In fact, we get on very well together. The only thing is that—he's—a woman.

GRIMSDYKE (*highly alarmed*) A woman! (*Recollecting*) Sleeping in *my* room?

(SIMON *nods ruefully*)

(*Continues in a much fruitier voice*) That could be very handy.

SIMON (*alarmed at such instant interest*) When I say she's a woman, don't forget I mean a woman *doctor*. You know what *they're* like!

GRIMSDYKE. I dunno. I once had a very interesting afternoon with a microscope and a little blonde pathologist.

SIMON (*hurriedly*) I'm afraid you wouldn't be at all interested in Dr Barrington.

GRIMSDYKE. You mean she's got thick glasses and teeth like Ken Dodd's?

SIMON. No glasses, exactly. But she's rather an unfortunate young woman. Legs like a billiard-table's. And her personality! Like a bulldozer.

GRIMSDYKE. I rather look on forceful girls as a challenge.

SIMON (*very hurriedly*) It's worse than that.

GRIMSDYKE. I can't think of *much* worse. Unless she's got radio-active dandruff.

SIMON. It's a psychological problem. An unfortunate psychological problem. Very tragic. It occurs in young women from time to time. Even very attractive ones. You wouldn't find Nikki—that's Dr Barrington's name—in the slightest responsive to your advances. Or to anyone's advances. Even Dirk Bogarde's. Or James Bond's. She just isn't—well, switched on in that direction.

GRIMSDYKE (*sombrely*) You mean she's a case of congenital psychological frigidity?

SIMON (*nodding sorrowfully*) I'm afraid so. (*Moving below Grimsdyke to the desk*) An iceberg. And she's really such a nice girl. It's an awful pity.

GRIMSDYKE. It's an awful waste. (*A thought occurring to him*) How did you make the diagnosis?

SIMON (*flustered*) From—er—books.

(*The telephone rings.* SIMON *grabs it*)

Dr Sparrow speaking. . . . No, I wasn't asleep. I wasn't even in bed . . . Yes, I know late hours are bad for me . . . Who's that? . . . Oh! (*His tone becomes much politer*) Good evening, Lady Forcebrace . . . The Field-Marshal is laid low? . . . Regimental dinner. H'm. Well, it could have been that devilled lobster, I suppose. Has he had any emesis? . . . No, that's not an item on the menu, I mean has he—er—thrown up? . . . Very well, I'll be along straight away . . . No, just don't give him any drugs. Leave him in peace with a glass of water and a receptacle. (*He puts down the telephone*)

(NIKKI *hurries in* L)

NIKKI. Simon, I heard the phone . . . (*She pulls up short, seeing Grimsdyke*)

SIMON (*very awkwardly*) Grim—this is—er, Dr Barrington. Nikki—Dr Grimsdyke.

NIKKI (*advancing into the room, smiling*) We've already met.

GRIMSDYKE (*moving towards Nikki, surprised*) Have we?

NIKKI (*casually*) I just saw you asleep in my bed.

SIMON (*through clenched teeth, to Grimsdyke only*) You were *in* her bed! You swine!

GRIMSDYKE (*to Simon only; matter-of-fact*) Well, if she's frigid it doesn't matter, does it?

SIMON. It's bloody unhygienic.

NIKKI. What was the call, Simon?

SIMON. The Field-Marshal's been overstuffing himself again. I'd better go round, I suppose. If I don't jump to it he always looks as though he wished he'd got a firing-squad handy.

NIKKI. What a pity—after our lovely evening out. Even if there's been rather a lot of excitement since.

GRIMSDYKE (*noting this remark, smiling*) You took *our* partner out to dinner, did you, Simon? (*To Nikki*) I hope, Nikki, *only* because he thought you might be suffering from malnutrition?

SIMON (*quickly*) I felt Nikki was entitled to a little relaxation. She's been working terribly hard.

GRIMSDYKE (*taking no notice of this remark, facing Nikki*) Where did he take you? The old Country Club? Tsk, tsk. *Rather* lacking in imagination. That new place they've opened at the end of the by-pass—*much* more intimate. Do you shake?

NIKKI. As a matter of fact, I do.

SIMON. Nikki is extremely good at all dances.

(GRIMSDYKE *takes no notice—starts doing the dance. He so amuses* NIKKI, *she laughingly joins in*)

She has a natural sense of rhythm!

GRIMSDYKE (*still taking no notice*) You know—(*laughing*)—it was a bit of a giggle me getting into your bed.

(SIMON *is starting to look furious*)

NIKKI. Well, Dr Grimsdyke . . .

GRIMSDYKE (*huskily*) Call me Gaston.

NIKKI. Well, Gaston, *I* thought it a bit of a shock.

GRIMSDYKE. What do I look like while I'm asleep?

NIKKI (*smiles*) Perhaps it would be kinder not to say.

GRIMSDYKE. No, go on. Be cruel. I won't mind.

NIKKI. Rather like a patient after a major operation.

GRIMSDYKE (*not put out*) What a shame! I thought I had a sort of classical dignity in repose.

SIMON (*painfully, trying to cut in*) Grim, I think that Nikki's very tired . . .

GRIMSDYKE (*taking no notice*) I'm sure I've seen you somewhere before. Awake instead of asleep. I expect you get around an awful lot—Ascot, Henley, Wimbledon, Lord's?

NIKKI. I don't get around to *those* places.

GRIMSDYKE. Well, the Mecca, ten-pin bowling, wimpy bars, and bingo?

NIKKI. That's more like it!

SIMON (*who has been trying to edge into the conversation desperately, now putting himself between them. To Grimsdyke*) It's getting late. It's getting very, very late!

NIKKI (*concerned*) Simon, hadn't you better hurry into some clothes and see the Field-Marshal?

SIMON (*remembering*) The Field-Marshal . . . !

GRIMSDYKE. You'd better run along, old lad. You'd never live it down if the victor of Uzzi Waddi succumbed to an impacted fish-bone.

SIMON. Grim, you go and see him.

GRIMSDYKE (*pointing out the obvious*) Oh, come. You know how he reacted when I simply bumped into him on the golf course. (*To Nikki*) How did I know he was behind that bush?

SIMON (*desperately*) Nikki—you go.

NIKKI (*dutifully, screwing her hands up*) Of course, Simon, if you're very tired—but—well, the Field-Marshal wouldn't take kindly to a *lady* doctor after sixty solid years in the army.

GRIMSDYKE (*dignified, and protective of womanhood—putting his arm round Nikki's waist*) Simon, I am surprised at you. Trying to send this charming girl out—at an hour like this—to do your dirty work with a drunken soldier.

(SIMON's *reaction to this, particularly the arm, is one of confusion and desperation. But he sees he must give in*)

SIMON. All right! All right! I'll go and see the Field-Marshal. I'll sit up and hold his hand all night, if that's what he wants!

(SIMON *pulls Grimsdyke's arm from Nikki and makes for the door up* R)

GRIMSDYKE (*hurriedly, in a low voice to Simon*) I say, old lad—couldn't manage a fiver's advance on next week's salary, could you?

SIMON (*loudly*) No!

(SIMON *exits* R, *slamming the door*)

GRIMSDYKE (*sighing*) Dear me! The poor fellow *does* seem to get into moods these days.

NIKKI (*pointedly removing the replaced protective arm and moving well away*) He's terribly, terribly sweet, Simon, isn't he?

GRIMSDYKE (*thoughtfully*) You think so? Yes, I suppose he is really quite a pleasant sort. Though rather inclined to be dull. It's going to be rather fun working with a lady doctor.

NIKKI. I'm sure you'll find it exactly the same as working with a male one. (*She backs away* L)

GRIMSDYKE (*advancing as Nikki backs away*) You are, I fear, far from right there. And the stupid thing is that Simon—the silly dolt—gave me the impression you were an absolute horror.

NIKKI (*stopping*) What?

GRIMSDYKE. He hasn't got an eye in his head! He said you'd got legs like a billiard-table—and had a personality like a bulldozer! Made you sound as if you resembled the back of a bus. And a pretty battered old bus at that!

NIKKI (*extremely displeased at the description*) I see.

GRIMSDYKE. But, of course, you mustn't take Simon too much to heart. The trouble is, he knows nothing whatever about women. Of course, he *thinks* he does. He's done a course of midder and gynae. He knows all about the female sex. You might as well say, you study the form-book and everyone's a winner. (*Advancing*) It's the practical, on-the-course experience that counts.

NIKKI. But he *couldn't* have said that! Not Simon . . .

GRIMSDYKE. In this very room. A few minutes ago. After describing a wonderful girl like you in such basic terms, he damn well ought to confine his practice to elderly Field-Marshals. And that's not all! (*Laughing*) He told me that you were—(*laughing*)—he told me you were frigid.

NIKKI (*furious*) He *did*, did he?

GRIMSDYKE. How misdiagnosed can you get!

(GRIMSDYKE *makes a grab at* NIKKI, *who pushes him away. Then* SIMON, *dressed normally, appears through the door* R, *behind Grimsdyke's back.* NIKKI *immediately throws herself into a highly passionate, lengthy embrace with* GRIMSDYKE. SIMON *looks on with amazement, horror, then rage. Finally, he grabs his bag, opens it, and throws some instruments in very noisily*)

(*Noticing Simon for the first time*) Oh, hello. I was just examining Nikki's tonsils.

SIMON. So I saw! (*Grabbing up his bag and making for the door up* L) I will leave you to your dalliance. (*Turning imperiously at the door*) Duty calls! *I*, at least, have some sense of obligation and decency.

(SIMON *exits* L)

GRIMSDYKE. Now he's out of the way, we can really get on with it. (*Making to embrace Nikki again*)

NIKKI (*pushing him away*) How tall are you, Dr Grimsdyke?

GRIMSDYKE. Oh—a bit under the six foot. (*He tries embracing her again*)

NIKKI (*pushing him away*) That's fine. Then you won't wake up in the morning with some complicated palsy of your feet. You might if they hung over the end.

GRIMSDYKE (*blankly*) The end of what?

NIKKI. The examination couch. You're going to sleep on it.

GRIMSDYKE. What, that?

NIKKI. Unless you want to walk round the surgery all night. (*Crossing Grimsdyke to* R) Or curl up with the cat behind the boiler. If you will please accompany me upstairs . . .

GRIMSDYKE (*eagerly*) Yes, of course.

NIKKI. I'll get you a pair of sheets from the linen cupboard.

GRIMSDYKE (*puzzled*) I don't get the message! (*He moves up* C)

NIKKI. There *is* no message—whatever.

(NIKKI *exits* R)

GRIMSDYKE (*standing beside the* AUTODOC; *speculatively, to himself*) Perhaps she is, really, after all?

(GRIMSDYKE *absently puts the* AUTODOC *into operation. The lights flash, bells ring, and with an enormous crash a torrent of silver coins fall from the chute. He looks surprised, then delighted with this jackpot, getting down to shovel it into his mac pocket. As he stands he looks at the machine very closely*)

I suppose I *did* get the right number in their catalogue?

(GRIMSDYKE *shrugs and leaves quickly by the door* R, *jingling loudly.* KITTEN *now enters up* L, *still in her nightie, carrying a pile of bedding, and looking disgruntled. She pulls back the curtain, eyes the examination couch, heaves a sigh, and makes her bed up on it. She snuggles down in it, and pulls the curtain round again.* GRIMSDYKE *enters* R *with a pair of sheets. He briskly pulls back the curtain round the couch.* KITTEN *sits up and screams*)

GRIMSDYKE (*amazed*) Kitten! Good heavens! You actually came for the job?

KITTEN (*pulling the bedclothes tight round her*) Go away.

GRIMSDYKE. But *I'm* supposed to be sleeping there.

KITTEN (*pulling the bedclothes tighter*) Only over your dead body.

GRIMSDYKE (*putting on the charm*) Oh, come along, Kitten . . .

KITTEN. You keep your distance! You don't want me to get out my judo, do you?

GRIMSDYKE. But this isn't the spirit of the Mecca, and the ten-pin bowling.

KITTEN. I've changed. My entire life—all changed. When you bought me them cashew nuts and said, "Come and be my nurse," you didn't think I'd take it on, did you?

GRIMSDYKE (*smiling shrug*) Well—it was just a little compliment.

KITTEN. You were wrong. I had always wanted to dedicate myself to succouring the sick and suffering. I've been at it now for a fortnight.

GRIMSDYKE (*frowning*) What exactly *do* you do?

KITTEN. Answer the telephone, file the notes, and hold the doctor's hand when he looks at naked women.

GRIMSDYKE. I suppose it's a start, anyway.

KITTEN. My past is a closed book. I am devoting myself in future to the wonderful advances in medical science.

GRIMSDYKE (*looking round*) Would you mind if I curled up on the floor?

KITTEN. I most certainly do mind!

GRIMSDYKE (*expostulating*) I'll take a double dose of sleeping pills.

KITTEN. I will not breathe the same night air as you, thank you very much.

GRIMSDYKE (*exasperated*) Then where *am* I going?

KITTEN. That's your problem.

(*Outside is the noise of a motor, and a honking of an old-fashioned bulb-horn.* GRIMSDYKE *and* KITTEN *stare at each other in alarm as the din becomes louder*)

GRIMSDYKE. Somebody's driving a car into the house!

KITTEN. It's a motor-bike. (*Getting hysterical again*) It's a ghost. That's what it is—a ghost. One of them ton-up boys what missed the corner at the end of the by-pass. Come back to haunt us. His leatherwork will be all luminous! (*Hysterical*) Oooo! I wish I hadn't come here at all. Oooo . . . !

GRIMSDYKE. Not hysteria, *please!*

(GRIMSDYKE *picks up a glass of water from the sterilizer shelf and tosses it in Kitten's face.* KITTEN *shuts up abruptly*)

(*Moving up* L) I'm going to have a pretty severe word with this joker. Doesn't know his Highway Code.

(*The main door flies open and in comes* Sir Lancelot, *in tweeds, a crash-helmet, and goggles. He is driving his invalid carriage. This is a luxurious plush-lined, fringe-canopied, Edwardian bath-chair, fully mechanized. There is an engine, gear and brake leavers, bulb horn, headlights and direction flashers in operation, number-plate, and any other gadgets thought suitable. A loud tartan rug is wrapped round his knees. The carriage chases* Grimsdyke *out of the way and halts in the centre of the stage.* Sir Lancelot *switches off the engine before removing his helmet and goggles*)

Sir Lancelot (*cordially enough*) Good evening.

(Grimsdyke *and* Kitten *stare at him*)

Grimsdyke, perhaps you would kindly introduce me to this young lady? Has she been left over from your evening surgery? Or is she queuing for the morning one, like they do outside Covent Garden?

Grimsdyke (*moving to* R *of Sir Lancelot*) Er—Miss Strudwick. Our nurse.

Sir Lancelot. Charmed.

Kitten. Coo.

Grimsdyke. This is Sir Lancelot Spratt, Kitten—Miss Strudwick. A professional colleague.

Sir Lancelot. I want heat. (*Throwing aside the rug*) Radiant heat. I have had a perfectly disastrous day. I lost a small fortune when the favourite let me down at Sandown Park. Then I suffered another attack of this blasted lumbago. Wouldn't respond to any damn treatment whatever. Even had my missus rubbing it with my best Napoleon brandy. Couldn't get a wink of sleep. The only thing I hadn't tried was radiant heat. Come on, Grimsdyke, don't stand there! The sum total of your professional abilities required is to press the switch. I presume you can do that without fusing the mains?

Grimsdyke (*leaping into action*) Yes, of course, sir. Let me help you on to the couch.

(Grimsdyke *struggles to get Sir Lancelot from the chair*)

Sir Lancelot (*loudly to Kitten*) Nurse! Lend the doctor a hand.

(Kitten *stays under her sheet*)

Grimsdyke (*struggling heavily, with Sir Lancelot on top of him*) Come on—this is one of the sick. Succour him.

(Kitten *gets off the couch, revealing her costume*)

Sir Lancelot. The nurse's uniform seems to have changed since my day. (*To Grimsdyke*) Be careful with my epicondyles, you fool!

(Kitten *and* Grimsdyke *manage to get* Sir Lancelot *on his face on the couch*)

KITTEN. Comfy?

SIR LANCELOT. Don't stand there, woman! Pull my shirt-tails up.

(KITTEN *bares his back as* GRIMSDYKE *wheels round the radiant heat lamp*)

GRIMSDYKE (*brightly*) How do you want it, sir? *Au point*, or rather overdone?

SIR LANCELOT. Stick it on the lowest voltage. And remember to switch it off again in ten minutes.

GRIMSDYKE. Right you are, sir. (*He switches on the lamp*)

SIR LANCELOT. Now leave me in peace. I want to get a few moments' shut-eye. I shan't be in a fit state to face the fish in the morning.

KITTEN. Who exactly is that bearded old . . .

GRIMSDYKE. Shhh! (*He drags her to the C of the room*) He's a very important gent.

KITTEN. Riding his scooter in the middle of the night, scaring the life out of decent people.

(SIMON *enters* L *with his bag. He pulls up short, seeing the carriage*)

SIMON. What the hell's this? (*Moving above the chair*) The Old Crocks' Race?

GRIMSDYKE. Shhh! Sir Lancelot dropped in for a dollop of radiant heat. (*He tiptoes to the curtain and peeps inside*) The old B's dozed off.

SIMON (*inspecting the carriage closely*) But what *is* it?

GRIMSDYKE. A sort of atomic-age bath-chair, I suppose.

SIMON. What are you doing out of bed, Kitten? And you, Grim. (*Remembering*) You lecherous bacterium!

GRIMSDYKE. With Nikki? But I was being strictly professional.

SIMON. I am glad that I, in such matters, have retained my amateur status.

GRIMSDYKE (*explaining patiently*) Simon—when you've made a diagnosis, what's the golden rule? Confirm it, whenever possible, with special investigations. That's exactly what I was doing. And your diagnosis was wrong! Completely wrong. She's defrosted and ready to serve.

SIMON. How dare you say . . . ! (*Suddenly resigning himself*) All right, we'll talk about it in the morning. When we've all had a bit of sleep.

KITTEN. Where?

GRIMSDYKE (*looking round*) You have a point. Ah! (*Noticing the telephone, he makes a grab for it and dials a number*) Hello? This is Dr Grimsdyke—Dr Sparrow's practice. Is that the Hampden Cross Memorial Hospital? . . . Good. Have you any empty beds? . . . Fine, I want to fill one . . . Yes, male. Don't bother about the diagnosis. The patient'll be along in a few minutes. (*He puts down the telephone and makes for the door* L) I'll put myself down as found wandering with loss of memory. Good night.

(GRIMSDYKE *exits* L)

Simon. What an evening! (*He sits disconsolately on the patient's chair*) I'm afraid Dr Barrington or I will have to leave. It had better be me. I'll find a ship—get a job as a doctor at sea.

Kitten (*tenderly, but not seductively, putting an arm round his shoulders*) Poor Dr Sparrow! Why don't you get it off your chest?

Simon. I'm afraid it would only bore you.

Kitten. No, honestly. Men always confide in me. You'd be surprised at some of the things.

Simon. It's really of no interest to anyone but myself . . .

Kitten. It'll make you feel better. Come on—tell the doctor everything.

Simon (*smiling and shrugging*) This very evening I took the most wonderful girl in the world out to dinner. I was screwing up courage so that afterwards I could ask her to marry me. Quite took my appetite away for the fruit salad and cheese board. Anyway, the operation was *not* successful. Funny, isn't it, Kitten—a chap starting a proposal never thinks he'll come out on the worst side. Any more than a chap starting a fight. I suppose if it occurred to them they'd steer clear of both. Oh, Nikki made all sorts of excuses. Her career —fair enough. Hadn't known me long enough—fair enough, too, I suppose.

Kitten. A girl likes to play hard to get. Though I reckon after a fortnight it becomes a bit of a strain.

Simon. No, *that* wouldn't be the game. Not with such an intelligent, balanced girl as Nikki. It's simply that she finds me crushingly dull. She didn't waste any time throwing herself into the arms of that moth-eaten Don Juan, Grimsdyke! Right in front of my eyes! Kissing her as though he'd been on a starvation diet for a month. *And* in her nightie!

Kitten. Do you read *Honey?*

(Simon *looks blank*)

It's a magazine.

Simon. I'm afraid I don't get much time for anything but the *Lancet.*

Kitten. It amazes me! I have to tell you doctors—who've read shelves and shelves of books, all in Latin and Greek—about the one thing you do not know—Life.

Simon (*smiling*) My dear Kitten! Where did you, in your few years, learn about it?

Kitten. Window-dressing. Listen—(*emphatically*)—she loves you.

Simon. Rubbish!

Kitten. Of course she does! She's been going round looking half-stunned with love all the last week.

Simon. But if she loves me, why was she—voluptuzing with Grimsdyke?

Kitten. Ain't you heard of the green-eyed monster?

Simon. But Nikki—a highly educated woman—wouldn't play a trick like that?

KITTEN. Go on with you! All women are the same when they're stripped for action.

SIMON (*blankly*) What shall I do?

KITTEN. Give her a great big sexy kiss and tell her she's hooked for life.

SIMON (*jumping up*) By God, Kitten, you're right. At least, I'll give it a try. If she hits me on the head with her patella hammer— (*He pauses and sniffs*)

(*Smoke, ever-thickening, starts to roll from the curtain*)

Did you leave anything on in the kitchen?

KITTEN. No.

SIMON. You sure?

KITTEN. Certain. That little fat fellow fussed turning everything off.

SIMON. That's odd. I'm sure I smell something like—overcooked meat.

KITTEN. Yeah. So do I.

(*By now the smoke is pretty dense. The diagnosis dawns on them. They both turn slowly and eye the curtain in horror*)

SIMON (*leaping forward*) Sir Lancelot . . . !

SIR LANCELOT (*appearing with a roar from the curtains, emitting smoke*) You, boy! You dolt! You cretin! You fool!

SIMON. I—er, I'm afraid the medicine was a little strong, Sir Lancelot.

SIR LANCELOT. Don't stand there gibbering. (*Running* RC *and back to* LC) Extinguish me, man, extinguish me!

SIMON. Yes, of course, Sir Lancelot . . . (*He looks round hopelessly*)

KITTEN (*grabbing a blanket from the couch and wrapping it round Sir Lancelot*) Here you are, duckie.

SIR LANCELOT. Thank God someone in the house is possessed of sense!

KITTEN. I learnt it in the Brownies. (*She moves* RC)

(WILDEWINDE *rushes in* L *with a large red fire-extinguisher*)

WILDEWINDE (*running down* C) Fire! Fire! Where's the fire?

SIR LANCELOT. Not *that*, you moron! I'm not the blasted kitchen flue.

SIMON (*grabbing the extinguisher, with Wildewinde*) Are you sure, sir? We want to make quite certain you're out.

SIR LANCELOT (*roaring*) Put it down!

SIMON. Yes, sir.

(WILDEWINDE *and* SIMON *drop it. Foam goes everywhere, particularly over Sir Lancelot and Wildewinde.* KITTEN *finally puts her finger on th nozzle, stopping the flow*)

SIR LANCELOT. I'll report you to the General Medical Council! I'll report you to the police!

SIMON. Sorry—it slipped.

SIR LANCELOT. You're not fit to be a doctor! You're not fit to run errands for Burke and Hare!

SIMON (*becoming angry*) There's no need to be so offensive. After all, I was trying to put you out.

SIR LANCELOT. Yes—after you'd set me on fire in the first place!

SIMON. Mistakes happen in the best regulated surgeries.

SIR LANCELOT. But not so bloody often as in this one!

SIMON (*drawing himself up defiantly*) Very well! If you don't like the service this practice provides, you needn't put up with it. I do *not* wish to have you as one of my patients, and under National Health regulations, I have the perfect right to get rid of you.

SIR LANCELOT. No-one could be more delighted than me!

SIMON. Your manners are about as ham-fisted as your surgery . . .

SIR LANCELOT. How *dare* you speak like that to me!

SIMON. Someone ought to have spoken like that to you years ago. It would save the world its most painful case of megalocephaly—big-headedness.

SIR LANCELOT. I shall inform my solicitors! I am suing you for slander! For astronomical damages . . .

SIMON. Go ahead. At least I shall never have to look at your bristling, bloated features again as long as I live! Wildewinde—(*imperiously indicating the desk*)—fetch me Sir Lancelot's health card.

WILDEWINDE (*very outraged and very foamy*) I shall not fetch Sir Lancelot's health card, Doctor! I have resigned. I have never known such disgraceful goings-on in a medical establishment. I shall leave in the morning. (*Making for the door* L, *tragically*) My lovely new pyjamas!

(WILDEWINDE *exits* L)

SIMON. Kitten—fetch me Sir Lancelot's health card.

(KITTEN *goes to obey, releasing the foam, which covers Sir Lancelot even more luxuriously.* NIKKI, *in her dressing-gown and nightdress, enters* R *anxiously*)

NIKKI (*moving* C) Simon! The house is on fire!

SIMON (*running up* C *to Nikki*) It doesn't matter about that. Will you marry me?

NIKKI. Of course I will, darling. Shouldn't we send for the fire brigade?

SIMON. Darling Nikki!

NIKKI. Darling Simon!

(NIKKI *and* SIMON *embrace. The foam gradually stops.* SIR LANCELOT *stands immobile, past resistance.* KITTEN *stands down* RC *holding out a buff card to him*)

SIMON. Darling, I wanted to marry you as soon as I set eyes on you.

NIKKI. Darling, so did I.

SIMON. We'll get married in—oh, next month?
NIKKI. As soon as you like.
SIMON. We'll have an enormous cake.
NIKKI. And lots of terrible presents.
SIMON. Champagne . . .
NIKKI. Speeches . . .
SIMON. You can come into the practice now!
NIKKI. Of course! To hell with psychology.
SIMON. To hell with it! We'll buy a lovely little cottage.
NIKKI. With a thatched roof. And a twisted chimney.
SIMON. A pretty garden—not too big.
NIKKI. With roses.
SIMON. And strawberries. Our children will be brilliant.
NIKKI. And terribly attractive.
SIMON. When they grow up I'll retire and start fishing.
NIKKI. I'm for embroidery.
SIMON. What a life!
NIKKI. What a life!

(NIKKI *and* SIMON *laugh happily.* NIKKI *then catches sight of the smouldering and foaming Sir Lancelot. In a matter-of-fact tone*)

Oh, hello, Uncle. (*Moving down* C) Paying a call?
SIMON (*horrified*) Uncle! (*He moves down* R *of Nikki*)
NIKKI. Yes, didn't I tell you? I haven't got any parents and Lancelot's my guardian. He was my contact with St Swithin's. That's how I got this job.
SIMON. Uncle!

(*All four exchange glances*)

SIR LANCELOT (*with intense menace*) Come along, Simon—give your new nunky a great big kiss.

CURTAIN

ACT III

SCENE—*The same. Morning, a month later.*

The room is now restored to its appearance at the start of the play, except that there are flowers on the desk—different from those in Act II. On the window-seat is a grey top hat.

When the CURTAIN *rises,* KITTEN *is discovered standing* C, *dressed as a bridesmaid—a rather unconventional one in a flashy, low-cut dress with a very short skirt. She is holding a small posy, and sobbing. The door up* L *opens, revealing* SIMON, *in morning dress, but with his trousers over his arm. Seeing Kitten, he rapidly retires.* KITTEN'S *sobs increase in intensity, until* SIMON *reappears and enters, properly dressed. He is naturally in a jubilant mood, though his trousers reach several inches over his ankles.*

SIMON (*moving to* L *of Kitten*) Hello, Kitten. Why the waterworks? This is the happiest day of *my* life, anyway.

KITTEN (*stopping crying and sniffing instead*) Weddings always make me cry.

SIMON. Oh, come. Just think of those nice, handsome—as yet unmarried—doctors I've asked. All looking at you in church.

KITTEN. I'm only the bridesmaid. They won't look at *me*.

SIMON (*inspecting her*) I wouldn't be too sure of that. (*Crossing* R *to rummage in the instrument cupboard*) Where's the adhesive strapping?

KITTEN. Have you hurt yourself?

SIMON. No, it's these damn trousers. The people in the clothes-hire emporium seem to think I suffer from pituitary gigantism. (*He produces a reel of strapping and, turning up his trousers inside, sticks them in place with it. Smiling*) Come on, Nurse! Scissors. (*He moves* RC)

(KITTEN, *still holding her posy, moves down* R, *briskly taking scissors from the sterilizer shelf and cuts the strapping on one trouser leg.* SIMON *starts sticking the next one*)

Perhaps I flattered myself thinking your tears, my dear Kitten, were because this very day you're leaving our little establishment.

KITTEN. It's a wrench, I don't mind telling you.

SIMON. And for us. Let me say you have the qualities of a splendid nurse—poise, charm, keeping your head in all emergencies. But I think your decision to leave was right. It is a little dull here. You'll be much happier in your new job behind the bar at the *Hat and Feathers.* Cut!

(KITTEN *snips the other strip of adhesive strapping. He is now reasonably smart*)

Besides, you can always discuss clinical matters in the richest detail with Mr Wildewinde. He's in the *Hat and Feathers* every night these days.

KITTEN. Good job he left, I suppose. (*Indicating the couch*) Wouldn't like to have kipped on that thing for the last month. (*Tidying away the strapping and scissors*) I hope he likes *his* new job.

SIMON (*moving up* C) He's a tremendous success! (*Putting on the top hat*) I met his boss only yesterday afternoon, on—er, professional matters. He reckons Wildewinde was born to it.

KITTEN. I reckon it's unhealthy. Being an undertaker's assistant.

SIMON. Anyway, this morning, we're concentrating on weddings.

(KITTEN *at once bursts loudly into tears*)

SIMON (*moving down* R) Come on, Nurse! *You* need a stimulant. Get me a couple of medicine glasses.

(SIMON *produces from the dressing-bin a bottle of champagne.* KITTEN *stops crying and produces two medicine glasses from the instrument cupboard.* SIMON *opens the champagne with a pop and pours it. Before he can drink any champagne the telephone rings*)

(*Moving to the desk, putting the bottle on it*) Even on your wedding day! (*Into the telephone*) Dr Sparrow here . . . Oh, the Memorial Hospital. Yes, what can I do for you? (*His face falls as he listens*) Oh . . . Oh . . . Dr Farquarson . . . A relapse while out on his rounds . . . You've got him in the ward now, have you? Good . . . Yes . . . Probably nothing serious, I agree, but best to take precautions. I expect he *is* struggling to get back to work, but you keep him in bed. (*With a slight smile*) Yes, it is, as a matter of fact. We're due at the church in about an hour. We'll fix things up somehow. We don't want Dr Farquarson to perforate. Tell him we're both thinking of him, and we'll come and see him as soon as we can. (*He puts down the telephone with a look of great anxiety*) Damn! My fault, I suppose. Obliging him to come back to work so soon. But it's awkward. He was going to hold the fort for everyone.

KITTEN (*putting the glasses on the desk*) Couldn't you get one of the other doctors in the town?

SIMON (*moving up* C) They're all coming to the wedding. (*Puzzling*) I suppose I could get the G.P.O. to put calls through to the church. It would sound a bit odd, wouldn't it, "Do you, Nichola, take this man Simon to be your lawful wedded husband, and Mrs Smith's little boy's got a nasty case of earache?" (*He sits disconsolately on the window-seat*) Nikki and I were resigned to having a week-end's honeymoon. Now it looks as if it's going to be an afternoon. (*Glancing through the window*) I only hope it keeps fine for us.

KITTEN. Perhaps Dr Grimsdyke will think of something bright? He always does.

SIMON (*looking at his watch*) Where the hell *is* he? It's all right for the bride to be late, but not the best man. He's probably drinking in every pub on the way from London. I'd better tell Nikki of the

Farquarson crisis. How's she getting on?

KITTEN. Still dressing in her room when I left her.

SIMON. Ask her if she'll come in when she's ready, will you?

KITTEN (*horrified*) What, see your bride actually before the wedding? It's unlucky!

SIMON (*resignedly, removing his top hat*) I'm afraid, Kitten, superstition and medicine don't mix.

(KITTEN *makes for the door up* L, *which bursts open to reveal a jubilant* GRIMSDYKE, *in morning dress*)

GRIMSDYKE. "For I'm to be married today, today. Yes, I'm to be married today!" Hello, old lad! Which side are you going to hold your orange blossom? (*Eyeing Kitten*) That's a pretty fetching line of nuptial rig!

(KITTEN *tosses her head and exits* L. GRIMSDYKE *gives her a pat on the behind as she passes him*)

Champagne! (*Moving to the desk*) Decent of you to have the bottle open and ready. (*He takes a glass*)

SIMON (*gloomily*) Farquarson's duodenum's blown up again. There's no-one to stand in for us during the ceremony.

GRIMSDYKE (*drinking and refilling his glass*) Oh. Nobody's going to be ill on a nice morning like this.

SIMON. Don't you believe it! Nikki and I went to the races last Saturday. When we got home there was a visiting list as long as your arm. *I* don't want to get hauled before one of those National Health disciplinary committees. To be told off like a naughty schoolboy, because some disgruntled patient's had to miss his bingo, waiting for you to come and see his sore foot.

GRIMSDYKE (*lightly*) We'll think of something. Anyway—(*sitting with his glass in the doctor's chair and putting his feet on the desk*)—after the wedding, of course, I'm taking over for the night.

SIMON (*rising and moving above the desk,* L *of Grimsdyke*) You *are* free for the week-end?

(GRIMSDYKE *nods*)

It's odd to think, Grim, if it weren't for you we wouldn't get a honeymoon at all.

GRIMSDYKE. Where are you going for it?

SIMON. We've found a quiet little pub in Devon.

GRIMSDYKE. You're not signing yourself as "Doctor and missus", I trust? A mistake, I assure you. I remember one of the lads from St Swithin's did that. They'd no sooner retired for the night than there was a terrible hammering on the bedroom door—the landlord, saying the cook had broken her ankle and would the doctor come at once. The marriage was consummated, but only just.

(KITTEN *enters* L)

KITTEN. Nikki'll be down in a minute, Simon. And there's four people in the waiting-room.

SIMON (*banging the desk in exasperation*) Blast them! This really strains the Hippocratic oath at the seams! Who are they?

KITTEN. There's Mr Pelly with his injections . . .

SIMON (*angrily*) He should have come yesterday.

KITTEN. And Mrs Evans with her chest . . .

SIMON. She should have come *tomorrow* . . .

KITTEN. And Mr Claribold.

SIMON. At least he's probably come about the house.

GRIMSDYKE. You found the dream cottage?

SIMON. An expensive dream!

KITTEN. And there's a lady what's come in response to your advertisement for a resident nurse.

SIMON. That's a bit of good news, anyway! What's she like?

KITTEN. Very presentable, I'd say.

SIMON. Young? Old? White? Coloured?

KITTEN. A young white lady. Well dressed.

SIMON. Show her in.

GRIMSDYKE (*rising and moving up* L) I'll go and get your wedding present from the car.

(KITTEN *exits* L, *followed closely by* GRIMSDYKE, *who manages to administer a few more playful pats.* SIMON *spots the champagne bottle and glasses and picks them up, looking for somewhere to hide them, moving up* C. KITTEN *re-enters*)

KITTEN. Miss Florence Nightingale.

(SIMON *drops the bottle and glasses.* FLORENCE NIGHTINGALE *enters* L. *She is a pretty, poised, smartly dressed young woman, all smiles. She comes bounding in with arms outstretched.* KITTEN *slips out again*)

FLORENCE. I *knew* you'd be surprised to see me! Dear old Simon! You haven't changed a bit in all these long six months!

(FLORENCE *throws her arms round him and kisses him.* SIMON *is paralysed in all muscles*)

But aren't you pleased I've come?

SIMON (*disentangling himself very smartly*) Y-y-yes, of course, Sally.

FLORENCE (*smiling*) Well! You'd think I was incubating smallpox!

SIMON. Er—quite—yes—but not in the surgery.

FLORENCE (*inspecting his costume*) Simon, you must be doing splendidly well! I thought the only doctors who still went about in those sort of clothes made absolute fortunes, with Rolls-Royces and knighthoods.

SIMON. Rather—old-fashioned practice, you know.

FLORENCE. Is it single-handed? Or have you got a partner?

SIMON (*with a look of panic upwards*) Why—why did you come? Today of all days?

FLORENCE (*crossing below Simon to the desk*) Nothing like being first in the queue when you're after a job. (*Perching herself on the desk, showing a lot of leg*) I read your advertisement in the *Nursing Mirror* this morning, and being one of the unemployed I came straight down.

(SIMON *moves down* C *and makes a hopeless noise*)

What did you say?

SIMON. Nothing. Just a—touch of indigestion.

FLORENCE. Poor Simon! I hope your liver's all right again? I can see you now—lying there looking like a rather disgruntled Chinaman. But you were a very sweet patient. Do you remember you used to pretend you were too weak to hold your good night cup of Horlicks—so I had to help you? Just so you could hold my hand?

(SIMON *makes another noise*)

And when I smoothed your pillow in the darkness you made a great grab and kissed me?

SIMON (*horrified*) Did I?

FLORENCE (*laughing*) Don't let it worry you! I was delighted. It showed you were getting your strength back. And I was *most* flattered when they kept you in the ward that extra week—because not only your *pulse* went up when I took it, but your *temperature*, too!

SIMON (*totally hopeless*) Oh, dear!

FLORENCE (*more coyly*) And do you remember, Simon—at that New Year's hospital party?

(SIMON *covers his face with his hands*)

On the stroke of midnight you not only kissed me distinctly, but actually proposed marriage! (*She laughs gaily*)

SIMON (*leaping into action*) What happened to him? The other chap?

FLORENCE (*surprised*) What other chap?

SIMON. The millionaire sheikh. With the datestones.

(FLORENCE *looks very puzzled*)

The one you went off with. To the—oil-rich deserts of Arabia, or whatever they are.

FLORENCE. I must confess I don't know any sheikhs. Even poor ones.

SIMON (*puzzled*) We all heard at St Swithin's you'd eloped.

FLORENCE (*laughing*) *That* was the scandalous story, was it? I suppose I deserved it. Perhaps it was better than the truth. Particularly if he happened to be a *handsome* sheikh as well.

SIMON (*looking at her closely, very puzzled*) Then why *did* you walk out of St. Swithin's?

FLORENCE. I didn't walk out. I was pushed. Fired. And with a Matron's reference that reads like something out of *Fanny Hill*.

SIMON. But that old battle-axe of a sister said you were one of the best nurses in the ward!

FLORENCE. Alas, I was thrown out for moral reasons.

SIMON. Impossible!

FLORENCE. Your idea of morals and the Matron's are perhaps different. You don't have to be a scarlet woman to incur her displeasure, you know. Not even a shocking pink one. (*After a pause; more sombrely*) She sacked me because I was getting too friendly with the patients.

SIMON (*hotly*) I never saw you being in the slightest friendly with *any* patient! Oh! (*His voice tails off*) You mean . . . me?

FLORENCE (*sadly*) I'm afraid so, Simon. You were the innocent culprit.

SIMON. I'm most terribly, terribly sorry . . .

FLORENCE (*brightly again*) Anyway, as I've got such a stinking reference and can't get another job, I thought you could make up for it nicely by installing me here.

SIMON (*unthinkingly*) Of course, Sally! That's the very least I can do. You can start just as soon as you . . . (*His position strikes him*) Errrk! I must consult my partner.

FLORENCE. Is he in the house at the moment?

SIMON (*flying to the window and flinging it up*) Grimsdyke! Grimsdyke!

(GRIMSDYKE *appears at the window*)

GRIMSDYKE (*looking worried*) What's the matter, old lad? Another fire?

SIMON (*to Florence*) My partner, Dr Grimsdyke.

FLORENCE (*rising and moving up* R) Dr Grimsdyke! From St Swithin's.

SIMON (*to Grimsdyke*) *This* is Miss Florence Nightingale.

(GRIMSDYKE *tries to disappear, but* SIMON *grabs him. Holding a huge and ugly vase,* GRIMSDYKE *climbs in*)

FLORENCE. Well! Don't you bother about doors?

SIMON (*standing* R *of Grimsdyke*) Patients waiting out there—might buttonhole him and talk—you know . . .

FLORENCE. What on earth's that thing for?

GRIMSDYKE (*somewhat demoralized*) It's—er—for specimens.

FLORENCE. Rather decorative specimens you go in for in this practice?

SIMON (*quickly*) Private patients' specimens, of course.

FLORENCE. You're a smart-*looking* pair of doctors, anyway. I don't think I'm nearly classy enough for you.

SIMON (*to Grimsdyke*) Sally's after our job of resident nurse.

FLORENCE (*to Grimsdyke*) But I'm not after it any longer.

(SIMON *and* GRIMSDYKE *look relieved*)

(*Moving down above the desk*) Dear sweet Simon has just this minute appointed me.

(GRIMSDYKE *nearly drops the vase, but* SIMON *just manages to save it. They end up closely face to face over it*)

GRIMSDYKE. You've chosen a fine moment to get an attack of polygamy, haven't you?

SIMON. Get her out of the way. (*To Florence*) I'm a—little busy, this morning. Important consultation in—about half an hour's time. My partner will instruct you in your duties. It'll be more pleasant, I think, in the garden.

GRIMSDYKE (*pressingly*) Yes, the flowers are looking lovely.

FLORENCE. But think of my hay-fever!

SIMON. They're non-allergic flowers.

GRIMSDYKE. We get them specially.

SIMON. From Japan.

FLORENCE. What will you doctors think of next!

SIMON. I wish to God I knew!

FLORENCE (*crossing below the others to the door up* L) Very well, the garden if you insist.

SIMON (*running below Grimsdyke and grabbing her*) Not that way!

FLORENCE. You mean, through the *window?*

SIMON. Yes. Those patients out there. A nasty case of measles.

FLORENCE (*making for the door*) I've had it!

SIMON (*stopping her*) You can get it again, you know.

GRIMSDYKE. The second attack's always worse.

SIMON. *Very* nasty.

GRIMSDYKE. Often fatal.

FLORENCE (*shrugging*) Oh, well. If I ruin my nylons, Simon— (*patting his cheek*)—I want a nice new pair in my first pay packet. Fifteen denier. You *know* my size.

(GRIMSDYKE *and* FLORENCE *exit by the window,* SIMON *helping. They have hardly disappeared before* NIKKI *enters* L. *She is in full wedding rig, with her veil up. Her dress is one of the short kind.* SIMON *hears her enter and spins round with his back to the open window, looking horrible*)

NIKKI (*pulling up*) Darling! What on earth's the matter?

SIMON. It was a little stuffy in here.

NIKKI. Are you feeling all right?

SIMON. Fine. Splendid. (*Mopping his brow*) Wonderful. Do I look unusual?

NIKKI. You look as if you'd just done the great train robbery all by yourself.

SIMON. Perhaps I'm a little overcome. Emotion.

NIKKI (*taking him in her arms*) Poor Simon! A wedding's much more of a strain for the strong sex, isn't it?

SIMON. This one is, anyway.

NIKKI. It'll soon be over. She looks absolutely sweet, doesn't she?

SIMON (*jumping several feet*) Who?

NIKKI. Kitten, of course. I see the dear little thing has already claimed her bridesmaid's kiss. Her lipstick's on your collar.

(Simon *rubs frenziedly with his handkerchief. She notices the vase*)

What on earth's that rococco spitoon doing?

Simon. It's Grimsdyke's wedding present.

Nikki. Oh, dear! I suppose we can always use it if Mr Claribold's plumbing breaks down. So the best man's arrived, has he?

Simon. Yes, he's out in the gar—he's slipped out for a pint.

Nikki. Trust him! Then what's the panic about?

Simon. I'm afraid I couldn't possibly tell you—oh! *That* panic. Dr Farquarson's been admitted to the Memorial Hospital with his duodenum. There's no-one to stand in for us.

Nikki. Oh, dear!

Simon. And there's four—three—patients queuing outside.

Nikki. How inconsiderate!

Simon. Mr Claribold, Mr Pelly's injections, and Mrs Evan's chest.

Nikki (*moving down* R *to the shelf*) I suppose we'd better cope with them, hadn't we? (*Sadly slipping a stethoscope round her neck and preparing a syringe at the sterilizer shelf*) After all, we have our vocation. The patient *always* comes first, I'm afraid.

Simon (*glancing at the window; eagerly*) I tell you what, darling— I'll take Mr Claribold in here, and you somehow manage the injections and chest in the waiting-room. It'll save time. (*He moves to the cupboard for an overall*)

Nikki. What a good idea!

Simon. Perhaps you'd better remove your veil?

(Nikki *laughs and takes off her headdress.* Simon *holds out the overall for her to slip into*)

One of Kitten's aprons will save your dress.

Nikki (*leaning back on him as he puts it on her*) Darling Simon, I love you more than anyone's loved anybody in the whole world.

Simon. And so do I, darling.

(*They kiss*)

Nikki (*dreamily*) After the wedding, we're going to be terribly, terribly happy.

Simon (*swallowing*) After the wedding!

Nikki (*smiling*) Despite Uncle Lancelot. (*Briskly*) Now I'd better run along and stick this in Mr Pelly's backside.

(Nikki *exits up* L *with stethoscope and syringe.* Simon *leaps for the window*)

Simon (*hoarsely*) Grim! Grim!

(Simon *scrambles out of the window.* Kitten *enters* L, *still with her posy. She looks surprised*)

Kitten (*shrugging*) Gone to spend a penny, I suppose. Nerves. (*She sees the vase and picks it up to tidy it away on the sterilizer shelf down* R)

(WILDEWINDE, *in morning dress, with black top hat, appears at the open window*)

WILDEWINDE. My heart's ease! My love! My passion flower!

KITTEN. Oh. It's you. (*She moves to the desk and puts her posy on it*)

WILDEWINDE. My beauty! My queen! My little floral wreath!

KITTEN (*tidying the desk; distantly*) What would you be wanting?

WILDEWINDE (*plaintively*) You know what I'm always wanting.

KITTEN. Yeah, but that apart?

WILDEWINDE. I've brought Dr Sparrow a little wedding present. I'll fetch it in.

KITTEN. Not *now*.

WILDEWINDE. Yes, yes! I'm coming.

KITTEN. I'm *busy*.

(WILDEWINDE *disappears from the window.* KITTEN *carefully looks at herself in the glass of the cupboard, and rearranges her hair to her satisfaction.* WILDEWINDE *bursts in up* L)

WILDEWINDE (*running above the desk*) Samantha! My dear . . .

KITTEN. Coo, you don't half look a treat. Been to Moss Bros?

WILDEWINDE (*put out*) These garments happen to be my working clothes. (*He moves away* C)

KITTEN (*still tidying*) Been working this morning?

WILDEWINDE. We're really quite busy for the time of year. But I *had* to get to Dr Sparrow's wedding. So I arranged things to fit in nicely with it. If I may boast a little, I am doing rather handsomely.

KITTEN. Are you on piecework? Or a flat rate?

WILDEWINDE. There is, alas, only one shadow on my happiness. Your indifference, Samantha, to yours truly. Ever since you floated into my orbit—like some beautiful, new, luminous spacecraft—the night Sir Lancelot caught fire—I have been besotted about you, Samantha. Totally besotted.

KITTEN (*still busily tidying*) That's very kind of you, I'm sure.

WILDEWINDE. You know how I've been coming back here, morning and evening surgery.

KITTEN. Yeah. Nettlerash.

WILDEWINDE. It wasn't nettlerash which brought me here. It was *you*. I fancy Dr Sparrow was getting rather tired of my case.

KITTEN (*moving round the desk to* R *of Wildewinde*) You'll be **more** comfy when I'm drawing your beer for you at the *Feathers*.

WILDEWINDE (*going on his knees*) I don't want you to draw my beer for me in a public house, Samantha. I want you to draw great draughts of happiness for me at home.

KITTEN (*after inspecting him for some time*) I don't follow.

WILDEWINDE. Will you marry me, Samantha!

KITTEN (*startled*) Oh! (*Flustered but flattered*) I'll have to think.

WILDEWINDE. I assure you I have a big future in the business. And we have such jolly times, you know, at our conventions. Besides, I'm a very good cook.

KITTEN. Well—er—(*she giggles*)—I'll think.

WILDEWINDE. Do, do, say you'll be mine?

(SIMON *comes in briskly* L, *looking worried*)

(*Rising and moving* R *of Simon*) Dr Sparrow—on this joyful occasion I would beg you to accept from your humble servant—recently resigned —this little contribution towards your future happiness. (*He hands him a slip of coloured paper*)

SIMON (*taking it distractedly*) What is it?

WILDEWINDE. A voucher. From my establishment. For you and your sweet wife. It entitles you both to perfectly free services, when the occasion arises.

SIMON (*stuffing it in his pocket, distractedly*) I'll look forward to it. Kitten, send in Mr Claribold, will you? I ought to be quaking in my pew by now, instead of tendering the suffering.

(KITTEN *exits up* L *bowed out by* WILDEWINDE, *who follows her*)

(*Through the window*) Grim! Where *are* you?

(SIMON *sits in the doctor's chair and holds his head in his hands. He picks up Kitten's posy and with a groan tosses it aside. The door* L *opens and* MR CLARIBOLD, *still clutching his bowler, comes nervously in*)

(*Resignedly*) Sit down, Mr Claribold. Have you come about my house or your headaches.

MR CLARIBOLD (*sitting in the patient's chair*) Both, as you might say, Doctor.

SIMON. Don't tell me you've found more dry rot in the soffits?

MR CLARIBOLD. No, your soffits, Doctor, enjoy, I am glad to say, good health. But I do not like the look of your fonds.

SIMON (*puzzled*) My *fonds?*

MR CLARIBOLD. Yes, Doctor. Here and there they are a bit crummy, if you will pardon the expression.

SIMON (*hopelessly*) Well—order a new set of fonds and screw them on.

MR CLARIBOLD (*giving a precise laugh*) Very funny, Doctor. But I fear I could not screw on a new set of foundations.

SIMON (*horrified*) Foundations? God! That'll be ruinous.

MR CLARIBOLD. Then how about your fylfots?

SIMON. Paint 'em red, white and blue.

MR CLARIBOLD (*making a note*) As you say, Doctor. Though they will give a—what you might call—slightly bizarre effect. Fylfots in those hues in the parlour.

SIMON. Mr Claribold, I am past caring. It is looking highly unlikely that I shall ever live in the house any way. I shall turn it into a charitable institution for unfrocked nurses.

MR CLARIBOLD. Turning to the cranium, Doctor . . .

SIMON. What's wrong with that? Oh, yours! But make it brief, will you? Just for today.

MR CLARIBOLD. I am delighted to say, that my condition now appears to be relieved.

SIMON (*jumping up*) Spendid! (*Indicating the door*) Well, we won't need to see you again, will we?

MR CLARIBOLD. But there is something else, on which I would value your esteemed advice.

(SIMON, *looking disgruntled, sits again*)

You see, Doctor, I have effected the cure, by matrimony—or the contemplation thereof.

SIMON. I'm delighted! (*Rising again*) Let me just wish you every happiness and say good-bye . . .

MR CLARIBOLD. I would like, Doctor, a frank talk.

SIMON (*puzzled*) What about?

MR CLARIBOLD. Sex.

(SIMON, *disconsolately, sits again*)

You see, I believe all intending partners should have a frank talk with their doctors beforehand.

SIMON (*resignedly*) I suppose it's all part of the National Health Service.

MR CLARIBOLD. Sex, as they say, is an important factor in marriage.

SIMON. Well—yes—but you shouldn't get too excited about it. I mean—well, yes. You see, in marriage there's a man and a woman of course. Later, possibly children. Nothing to it, really.

MR CLARIBOLD. I am naturally concerned about our relations, Doctor.

SIMON. Oh, I shouldn't think they'd mind if you had children a bit.

MR CLARIBOLD. I mean our sexual relations.

SIMON (*rising, struck by an idea*) Look—there's a very good book on it. What's it called *Simple Sex*, or *Reproduction and Recreation*, fully illustrated. Twelve and sixpence.

MR CLARIBOLD (*writing*) *Simple Sex*.

(GRIMSDYKE *enters* L)

GRIMSDYKE. Sorry! Didn't know you had a patient.

SIMON (*eagerly*) He's just going. (*Indicating to Mr Claribold to leave*) You'll find all you want to know in that. Absolutely all! It deals with every possibility.

MR CLARIBOLD (*rising and moving up* L) Very obliged, Doctor. I shall peruse it this very afternoon. May I bring my intended along? You might give *her* a frank talk, too?

SIMON (*following Mr Claribold*) Yes, yes. Any time you like.

(MR CLARIBOLD *exits* L)

GRIMSDYKE (*moving* C) What were you doing to him?

SIMON (*moving* L *of Grimsdyke*) Prescribing a book on sexual technique.

GRIMSDYKE. I hope it isn't the one I once gave a patient. The man turned up next morning very cross with a fractured ankle.

SIMON. What have you done with Sally? Hidden her somewhere? (*Eagerly*) Cut her throat?

GRIMSDYKE (*soothingly*) My dear Simon, calm down. (*Sitting on the edge of the desk*) I've done the trick. I've completely neutralized her. You're a sterling chap, but you don't know how to *handle women.* Nikki, I grant you. But not flibbertygibbets. Luckily, old Uncle Grimsdyke was on hand.

SIMON. You told her some outrageous lie, I suppose?

GRIMSDYKE. No, I told her the utter and complete truth. I took her down to the bus shelter and explained that you'd met your soul-mate, were marrying her in about ten minutes, and any idea of Sally moving in as a resident nurse was—clearly not on.

SIMON. How did she react? After all, it was only six months since I was suggesting exactly the same process to her.

GRIMSDYKE. You don't understand woman's romantic soul! She thought the whole story absolutely smashing. Brought tears to her eyes.

SIMON (*becoming hopeful*) She's just forgetting about this job?

GRIMSDYKE (*rising*) I have induced total amnesia about everything. By the time I'm standing in church wondering where the hell I put the ring, she'll be on the train back to London.

SIMON (*grasping his hand*) How can I ever thank you?

GRIMSDYKE. Don't mention it. The old pal's act, you know.

SIMON. Do you realize that I'm indebted to *you* for my entire life's happiness?

GRIMSDYKE. Oh, come . . .

SIMON. I shall always remember it. (*Moving down* R) Always! We shall get the children to pray for you. Every night. Twice on your birthday. (*Struck by a thought*) But Sally—she'll think me the dregs, won't she?

GRIMSDYKE. On the contrary, she's so starry-eyed with vicarious romance, she wants to wish you long life and happiness.

SIMON. Where is she?

GRIMSDYKE. Just outside. Posing as a patient.

SIMON (*nodding, looking doubtful*) Be sure the coast's clear.

(SIMON *sits at the desk.* GRIMSDYKE *moves to the door* L, *looks carefully outside, gives a whistle and makes an inviting gesture.* FLORENCE NIGHTINGALE *comes in, smiling sweetly.* GRIMSDYKE *stays in the room, shutting the door carefully*)

FLORENCE (*moving* C) Simon, you must think I'm *awful!* I couldn't have picked a worse moment, if I'd had all eternity to choose from.

SIMON. It was possibly a weeny bit awkward.

FLORENCE. Will you ever forgive me?

SIMON (*awkwardly*) No, it's *me* you ought to forgive.

FLORENCE (*to Grimsdyke*) There now! The same old sweet Simon. Always the picture of perfect gallantry.

GRIMSDYKE. That's his charm.

FLORENCE. Now I'm going straight back home, and I'll never come to haunt you again, not as long as I live.

GRIMSDYKE (*quickly*) Want a lift?

SIMON (*to Grimsdyke; firmly*) *You* are taking over *here*.

FLORENCE. I only wish you lots of happiness. I'm sure your wife is *very* charming. And very lucky.

SIMON (*preening himself slightly*) Well, you know . . .

FLORENCE. Anyway, it *is* quite a coincidence! And really very funny. I just couldn't resist telling it to your pretty receptionist, though I *did* make out I nursed your jaundice more dramatically than I did. I swore her to strict secrecy, of course.

GRIMSDYKE. Who, Kitten?

FLORENCE. Is that he name? The girl in the white coat.

(SIMON *leaps from the desk*)

SIMON. You—you told that to the—girl in the white coat?

FLORENCE (*startled*) I'm sorry. Was it really so terribly wrong?

(NIKKI *bursts in* L, *furious, with her syringe and stethoscope. She strips off her white coat, moving to Simon above the desk.* FLORENCE NIGHTINGALE *reacts with horror as she sees the wedding dress*)

SIMON. I can explain everything.

(FLORENCE *backs up* L)

GRIMSDYKE. Yes, he can explain everything. . . .

NIKKI (*putting down her instruments on the desk, pulling off her ring and throwing it at Simon*) There's your ring. No doubt you will put it in the sterilizer before giving it to the next one.

(GRIMSDYKE *moves* L *of Nikki*)

SIMON. But, Nikki! Sally here only nursed me when I was ill at St Swithin's.

NIKKI. Don't bother to give me the case history. I already have it.

SIMON. We were never alone together—were we, Sally? There were dozens of people in the ward. Many of them fully conscious.

(FLORENCE *moves* L *of Grimsdyke*)

NIKKI. I wouldn't mind *that*. But she says you've been consulting her for stimulating liver exercises ever since. *And* you were wild to marry her.

GRIMSDYKE (*trying to mitigate the circumstances*) That was at a New Year's Eve party. He was probably drunk.

NIKKI. This very day—on our wedding morning—half an hour before you were due to take me, in my innocence, to the altar— knowing full well that you and I would have to live here alone, with our house not ready and Dr Farquarson in hospital—you arranged to install . . . that woman . . . under my very nose! For liver excercises, I suppose? A nice little *menage à trois* for you. You don't want to go to a wedding. You want to go to a psychiatrist.

FLORENCE (*pathetically*) But I didn't even give him a blanket bath!

NIKKI. Luckily there are *some* decent people in the world. (*Continuing to Grimsdyke in a strained voice*) Dr Grimsdyke, how can I thank you enough?

(GRIMSDYKE *looks surprised, but flattered*)

It was you who by sensibly talking Miss Florence Nightingale out of accepting this grotesque position, saved my reputation and my sanity.

GRIMSDYKE (*more flattered*) After all, one does what one can to forestall these things.

NIKKI (*seriously, to Grimsdyke*) My entire lifetime's happiness—(*sharply, looking at Simon*)—I need hardly say, away from Dr Sparrow, as far as possible—depended on your natural integrity this morning.

GRIMSDYKE (*with heavy charm*) Sense of duty, you know—to a lovely lady like you.

NIKKI. If I may used an old-fashioned but very true expression, you are a picture of perfect gallantry.

GRIMSDYKE (*getting more intimate*) Do you think so? How terribly sweet of you, my dear. Of course Simon's a very decent sort at heart, but he doesn't really understand women.

NIKKI (*tragically*) And now—all I want to do—is drown myself in the sea of London. At once.

GRIMSDYKE. Would you like a lift?

NIKKI. Thank you. I would. Very much.

SIMON (*roaring*) Grim! What the hell do you think you're up to?

GRIMSDYKE. Sorry, Simon. Just forgot myself for the moment.

SIMON (*comforting her and tripping over the strapping from his trousers*) Nikki—*I'm* the doctor you're supposed to be marrying. Not him!

NIKKI. Doctors shouldn't marry other doctors. Doctors shouldn't marry at all.

SIMON (*desperately*) But if you'll only listen to me for half a minute I'll explain it was all entirely innocent.

NIKKI. You under-ripe Bluebeard! (*Slaps him hard*)

(NIKKI *bursts loudly into tears and moves down* L. FLORENCE NIGHTINGALE *bursts loudly into tears and moves down* R *of Nikki*)

GRIMSDYKE. Do you think we ought to give them some some butobarbitone? Calm them down.

SIMON (*loudly*) No! (*He moves* R *to below the desk*)

GRIMSDYKE (*moving down* R, *to* L *of Simon*) Remember, all women get a bit het-up and nervy on their wedding day.

SIMON. Shut up!

GRIMSDYKE (*hurt*) I was only trying to help.

(KITTEN *enters, crying loudly, and moves down* C, *followed by* WILDEWINDE)

KITTEN (*still crying*) I'm going to be married! To Edgar.

(*Howling,* KITTEN *and* WILDEWINDE *embrace.* SIMON *starts rummaging in the cupboard*)

GRIMSDYKE. What are you looking for?
SIMON. The strychnine!

(*There is a loud honking off, and* SIR LANCELOT, *in his carriage, comes through the door. He is wearing morning dress, plus his goggles and crash-helmet. He comes to a halt down* C, *between Wildewinde and Florence, and removes· goggles and helmet.* SIMON *moves down* R)

SIR LANCELOT. Still in time to give away the bride, I hope. I'd have been here half an hour ago if my blasted back hadn't let me down again, just as I was getting into my striped pants. Don't know how the devil I'll get down the aisle, but I'll manage somehow, even on my hands and knees. Everyone gathered ready, I see, for the joyous occasion. (*He slowly surveys the scene. He is puzzled*) What the hell's going on here? Are the Beatles dead, or something?
SIMON. Er, understandable emotion.
SIR LANCELOT. They'd better cheer up pretty quickly. Our car's due any minute.
SIMON. I'm afraid it—er, won't be needed. The wedding is off.
SIR LANCELOT. Of course it isn't off. I spent fifty quid on your present.
GRIMSDYKE (*abashed*) Nikki and Simon have had a little technical trouble, sir.
NIKKI (*crossing below Florence to* L *of Sir Lancelot, very tearful*) It's just that he . . . wants to marry the two of us—(*indicating Florence Nightingale*)—that's all.
SIR LANCELOT (*very menacing, beckoning with his finger to Simon*) Come here, you little pustule.

(SIMON *meekly crosses to* R *of Sir Lancelot*)

If you are intending to do the dirt on Nikki, I will remind you that I dandled her on my knee as a little child. So would you like to go out and walk under a bus? Or would you prefer to leave it to me to—(*roaring*)—break every bone in your blasted skeleton?
SIMON (*bursting out*) But I *don't* want to marry the two of them. I want to marry Nikki. Very, very much. (*He crosses below Sir Lancelot to* R *of Nikki*)
FLORENCE (*almost hysterical*) I don't want to marry *Simon.* I never did. And I don't want to see anyone in this place for ever and ever.
SIR LANCELOT (*eyeing her*) I know you. Florence Nightingale. I wangled you a job at St Swithin's. How's the baby?
NIKKI. Baby? Simon! (*She slaps him again*)
SIR LANCELOT. Must be growing up now.
FLORENCE. Yes—he's quite a little boy, thank you, Sir Lancelot.
SIR LANCELOT. Glad I was able to help with your hard luck story. I suppose you divorced that rotten husband in the end?

FLORENCE (*tearfully, in general*) You see, I wanted the job here because—it was living-in—so—I thought I could persuade Simon——being such a sweet man—that—later on—I could have my young son with me. And I'm getting married again soon. To a petty officer medical branch of the Navy, just being demobbed. I imagined he might move in, and perhaps be useful round the place.

SIR LANCELOT (*gruffly business-like*) There you are, Simon. You have not only found a wife but gained yourself another Wildewinde.

NIKKI (*to Florence; very eagerly*) It's true?

FLORENCE (*pathetically*) Can't you see?

NIKKI. Simon!

SIMON. Nikki!

(SIMON *and* NIKKI *embrace*)

GRIMSDYKE (*anxiously looking at his watch*) If the runners are sorted out, we'd better get down to the starting gate.

(*The telephone rings.* GRIMSDYKE *grabs it from below the desk*)

Dr Sparrow's surgery . . . Oh, God! (*He puts the receiver down again*) It's the Field-Marshal. He's sat on his sword.

SIMON (*desperately*) Who's going to look after the practice?

SIR LANCELOT. I can't, with a back like this.

NIKKI. Of course you can, Uncle. Jump to your feet. Jump! Jump!

(SIR LANCELOT *hesitantly obeys and finds, to his delight, he is normal*)

SIR LANCELOT. By God, how splendid! Now I can go fishing afterwards.

GRIMSDYKE (*to Nikki, amazed*) How did you do it?

NIKKI (*to Sir Lancelot*) It only came on in moments of stress, Uncle, didn't it?

SIR LANCELOT (*reflecting*) After a row with the missus, when I lost a fish, when I lost a lot of money, and tarting up for a wedding. Yes!

NIKKI. There you are! All mental. Even a *child* psychologist could tell you that.

SIR LANCELOT. Wildewinde!

WILDEWINDE. Sir?

SIR LANCELOT. You give the bride away. I'll tackle the Field-Marshal.

WILDEWINDE. Oo! Such an honour!

SIR LANCELOT. And if the slightest thing goes wrong, I'll break your neck.

GRIMSDYKE (*looking anxiously towards the window*) But no cars!

WILDEWINDE (*abashed*) I fear the cars are still engaged. I booked them earlier for one of my little functions. It must have gone on rather longer than intended.

SIMON. What are we waiting for?

(SIMON *grabs Nikki and seats her beside him aboard Sir Lancelot's carriage.* SIR LANCELOT, WILDEWINDE, KITTEN *and* FLORENCE *start to pull the carriage delightedly round the room, starting by wheeling down* L, *then turning, crossing down* R, *round* R *of the desk to up* C.

GRIMSDYKE *meanwhile picks up Simon's top hat and Nikki's head-dress*)
GRIMSDYKE. Your hats! You forgot your hats!

(*As the procession passes,* GRIMSDYKE *hands out the hat and head-dress which they put on,* NIKKI *covering her face.* GRIMSDYKE *then seizes a bag of confetti from the desk and throws it over them. As the company reaches up* C, *the door* L *opens and* MR CLARIBOLD *enters with a large book plainly marked* SIMPLE SEX)

MR CLARIBOLD. Doctor—may I present—my intended.

(MRS TADWICH *enters* L *and joins Mr Claribold*)

SIMON. Blimey, you're going to need that book!

CURTAIN

FURNITURE AND PROPERTY LIST

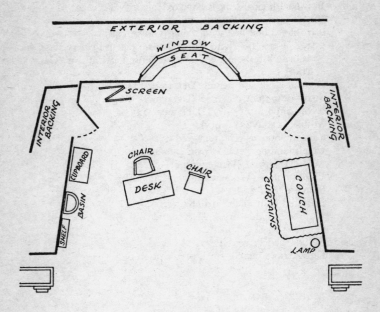

ACT I

On stage: Desk (RC) *On it:* 2 telephones, intercom with buzzer, writing
materials, large framed photograph, prescription pads, forms,
folders, lamp stand, stethoscope

Desk chair (behind desk)

Upright patient's chair (L of desk)

Window-seat (up C)

Surgical examination couch (L) *Round it:* curtains on runners

Screen (up R)

Surgery cupboard with mirror door (R). *In it:* books including
one heavy volume, dressings, instruments, medicine glasses,
overalls, adhesive strapping, bottles of pills

Wash-basin with surgical tap (below cupboard)

Shelf (down R). *On it:* electrical sterilizer, enamel dishes, instruments, scissors, folded overalls. *Under it:* doctor's bag, pedal-
operated dressings-bin.

Radiant-heat lamp with plug and wall socket (down L)
On door R: hook
On wall R *of window:* socket for AUTODOC electric plug
Carpet
Window curtains
Net curtains

Off stage: Buff health card (SIR LANCELOT)
Pile of unopened letters (WILDEWINDE)
Cardboard box tied with string (GRIMSDYKE)
2 large boxes tied with string. *In one:* electric ear syringe, transistorised stethoscope, dial with wires, head mirror (DELIVERY MAN)
Receipt book and pencil (DELIVERY MAN)
AUTODOC patent machine (DELIVERY MAN)
2 contemporary chairs (DELIVERY MAN)
Mobile (DELIVERY MAN)
4 plastic notices (DELIVERY MAN)
Creel, landing-net, rod (SIR LANCELOT)
Medical journal (WILDEWINDE)
Plastic notice (WILDEWINDE)
Suitcase (KITTEN)
National Insurance card (KITTEN)
Plate with ham sandwich (KITTEN)

Personal: SIMON: pencil, watch
GRIMSDYKE: pencil, card, prescription pad

ACT II

Strike: Parcels
Mobile
Notices
Medical journal
Photo from bin

Set: Furniture and props generally as at opening of Act I
AUTODOC up C
Vase of flowers on desk
Curtains closed
X-ray photos on desk
Glass of water on shelf down R
Health card on desk

Off stage: Bedding (KITTEN)
Sheets (GRIMSDYKE)
Invalid carriage (SIR LANCELOT)
Fire extinguisher (WILDEWINDE)

ACT III

Strike: Invalid chair
Fire extinguisher
Bedding
AUTODOC

Set: Furniture and props generally as at opening of Act I
Change flowers on desk
Grey top hat on window-seat
Scissors on shelf down R
Bottle of champagne in dressings-bin
Syringe and stethoscope on shelf down R
Overall in cupboard
Bag of confetti on desk

Off stage: Posy (KITTEN)
Vase (GRIMSDYKE)
Slip of coloured paper (WILDEWINDE)
Book titled *Simple Sex* (CLARIBOLD)

Personal: NIKKI: engagement ring
GRIMSDYKE: watch

LIGHTING PLOT

Property fittings required: pendant, desk lamp
    Interior. A consulting room. The same set throughout
    THE APPARENT SOURCES OF LIGHT are, by day, a window up C; by
      night, a pendant
    THE MAIN ACTING AREAS are RC, up C, down C, LC, up L, down L

ACT I. Morning
To open: Effect of summer morning light
No cues

ACT II. Night
To open: Room in darkness
Cue 1   NIKKI switches on lights   (Page 32)
           Snap on pendant and interior lighting

ACT III. Morning
To open: As Act I
No cues

EFFECTS PLOT

ACT I

Cue 1   Before CURTAIN rises   (Page 1)
Telephone rings, joined by second telephone, then by intercom buzzer

Cue 2   SIMON: ". . . this time it's different"   (Page 2)
Intercom buzzes

Cue 3   SIMON: ". . . the fire brigade"   (Page 2)
Intercom buzzes

Cue 4   MRS TADWICH: "And mine"   (Page 3)
Telephone rings

Cue 5   SIR LANCELOT: ". . . number of them do"   (Page 6)
Telephone rings

Cue 6   SIMON: ". . . off to Bournemouth"   (Page 6)
Telephone rings

Cue 7   SIMON: ". . . to the medical agencies"   (Page 7)
Telephone rings

Cue 8   SIMON: ". . . back to me"   (Page 10)
Telephone rings

Cue 9   SIMON: "Quite. Well . . .'   (Page 28)
Telephone rings

ACT II

Cue 10   SIMON exits   (Page 37)
Telephone rings

Cue 11   SIMON: "From—er—books"   (Page 41)
Telephone rings

Cue 12   KITTEN: "That's your problem"   (Page 45)
Motor horn

ACT III

Cue 13   SIMON opens champagne   (Page 53)
        Telephone rings

Cue 14   GRIMSDYKE: ". . . to the starting gate"   (Page 67)
        Telephone rings

MADE AND PRINTED IN GREAT BRITAIN BY
LATIMER TREND & COMPANY LTD PLYMOUTH